**Pr**

MW00979455

"It doesn't matter what your computer skill level is, this handbook will show you what you need to get moving in the OS X fast lane."

— Sean Alexandre, Bishop Eastern Sierra Macintosh User Group

"A very good roadmap through the latest version of the Mac operating system... I highly recommend it for your reference library. With its small size you can easily keep it on your desk, or slip it in a desk drawer."

— Rodney Broder, Mactechnics

"The book is richly illustrated, replete with tables, screen shots, hints and illustrations. These allow you to determine what/how to do in OS X the many tasks that were once 'routine and easy' from whatever system you've switched from. The 150 page 'Pocket-Guide' level book provides a straight-to-the-point 'primer' on working Mac OS X. This well written, exhaustively indexed, little guide book is highly recommended to anyone who is about to or recently switched to OS X."

— Harry (doc) Babad, *maccompanion.com*

"These mini Pocket Guides from O'Reilly answer almost all the essential questions... anyone with even minimal experience at Mac OS systems, old or new, will be using these handy guides often.... [Toporek's] got about 10 pages on basic Unix commands, for example, a subject I always start to glaze over when it comes up. But he gives the skinny with a clarity I could understand, and now I'm practically ready to be a superuser."

— Stephen M.H. Braitman, BOOK BYTES

# Mac OS X Panther
*Pocket Guide*

# Mac OS X Panther
## *Pocket Guide*

*Chuck Toporek*

# O'REILLY®

Beijing · Cambridge · Farnham · Köln · Paris · Sebastopol · Taipei · Tokyo

**Mac OS X Panther Pocket Guide**
by Chuck Toporek

Copyright © 2004, 2003, 2002 O'Reilly & Associates, Inc. The previous editions of this book were titled *Mac OS X Pocket Guide*. All rights reserved. Printed in the United States of America.

Published by O'Reilly & Associates, Inc., 1005 Gravenstein Highway North, Sebastopol, CA 95472.

O'Reilly & Associates books may be purchased for educational, business, or sales promotional use. Online editions are also available for most titles (*safari.oreilly.com*). For more information, contact our corporate/institutional sales department: (800) 998-9938 or *corporate@oreilly.com*.

| | |
|---|---|
| **Editor:** | Chuck Toporek |
| **Production Editor:** | Mary Brady |
| **Cover Designer:** | Emma Colby |
| **Interior Designer:** | David Futato |

**Printing History:**

| | |
|---|---|
| May 2002: | First Edition. |
| November 2002: | Second Edition. |
| November 2003: | Third Edition. |

Nutshell Handbook, the Nutshell Handbook logo, and the O'Reilly logo are registered trademarks of O'Reilly & Associates, Inc. The *Pocket Guide* series designations, *Mac OS X Panther Pocket Guide*, the image of a German shepherd, and related trade dress are trademarks of O'Reilly & Associates, Inc. Many of the designations used by manufacturers and sellers to distinguish their products are claimed as trademarks. Where those designations appear in this book, and O'Reilly & Associates, Inc. was aware of a trademark claim, the designations have been printed in caps or initial caps.

Apple, the Apple logo, AppleScript, AppleScript Studio, AppleTalk, AppleWorks, Aqua, Carbon, Cocoa, ColorSync, Finder, FireWire, iBook, iMac, Inkwell, iPod, .Mac, Mac, Mac logo, Macintosh, PowerBook, QuickTime, QuickTime logo, Rendezvous, and Sherlock are trademarks of Apple Computer, Inc., registered in the U.S. and other countries. The "keyboard" Apple logo (Option-Shift-K) is used with permission of Apple Computer, Inc.

While every precaution has been taken in the preparation of this book, the publisher and author assume no responsibility for errors or omissions, or for damages resulting from the use of the information contained herein.

0-596-00616-0
[C]

# Contents

# Part IV. Mac OS X Unix Basics

# Part V. Task and Setting Index

# Mac OS X Panther Pocket Guide

## Introduction

Last year, the big hype was Jaguar, and to some, Jag lived up to its hype by bringing a suite of new applications to Mac OS X, along with many improvements to the system itself. It booted faster, was more stable, and applications such as iChat and Address Book were soon followed by iCal, iSync, and updated versions of iMovie, iPhoto, and iDVD—all packaged together as a suite called *iLife*.

Now we're on to the next big thing: Panther (Mac OS X Version 10.3). Like its big-cat predecessor, Panther brings lots of improvements to the OS we all love so dearly. Some changes are subtle, such as a faster boot time, while others are drastic, but welcomed, such as a new and much-improved Finder and iChat AV, which brings audio and video chat capabilities to the Mac. At the system level, Apple has made lots of tweaks to the Unix layer that makes Panther purr. For most users, those system-level changes might not mean much, but that's the way it should be. You should be able to boot your Mac, install and run software, and have a great time.

This new edition of the *Mac OS X Pocket Guide* is intended to be a quick reference to Mac OS X Panther, and it has something for everyone:

- If you're an experienced Mac user, this book may be the only one you'll need. For Mac users coming to Mac OS X from an earlier version of the Mac OS, some of the material in this book can serve as a refresher, reminding you how to do certain things you've always been able to do on the Mac. In addition, you'll learn more about the Unix side of Mac OS X and how to use its command-line interface, the Terminal application.

- If you're a Unix, Linux, or FreeBSD user who is switching to the Mac, you'll get a quick summary of how to use Mac OS X's interface and how to use its Terminal application for issuing Unix commands. If you're looking for something more hardcore, I recommend that you pick up a copy of *Mac OS X Panther for Unix Geeks* (O'Reilly), which covers such things as Directory Services, use of Mac OS X's GCC compiler, installing packages with Fink, and running Apple's version of the X Window System.

- If you're a Windows user, you'll get a quick tour of the operating system, along with a guide to help you relate some Windows-specific terms to your Mac. While the Terminal and Unix commands will be all new to you, they're not too far off from the DOS prompt commands you've used in the past.

With over 250 tips and tricks, this *Pocket Guide* is a handy reference for configuring and working with your Mac OS X system.

# Conventions Used in This Book

The following typographical conventions are used in this book:

*Italic*

> Used to indicate new terms, URLs, filenames, file extensions, directories, Unix commands and options, and program names. For example, a path in the filesystem will appear as */Applications/Utilities*.

`Constant width`

> Used to show the contents of files or the output from commands.

---

**Constant width bold**

> Used in examples and tables to show commands or other text that should be typed literally by the user.

*Constant width italic*

> Used in examples and tables to show text that should be replaced with user-supplied values.

*Variable lists*

> The variable lists throughout this book present answers to "How do I . . ." questions (e.g., "How do I change the color depth of my display?"), or they offer definitions of terms and concepts.

*Menus/navigation*

> Menus and their options are referred to in the text as File → Open, Edit → Copy, etc. Arrows will also be used to signify a navigation path when using window options; for example, System Preferences → Screen Effects → Activation means you would launch System Preferences, click on the icon for the Screen Effects preferences panel, and select the Activation pane within that panel.

*Pathnames*

> Pathnames are used to show the location of a file or application in the filesystem. Directories (or *folders* for Mac and Windows users) are separated by forward slashes. For example, if you see something like "launch the Terminal application (*/Applications/Utilities*)" in the text, that means the Terminal application can be found in the *Utilities* subfolder of the *Applications* folder.

↵

> A carriage return (↵) at the end of a line of code is used to denote an unnatural line break; that is, you should not enter these as two lines of code, but as one continuous line. Multiple lines are used in these cases due to printing constraints.

$, #

> The percent sign ($) is used in some examples to show the user prompt for the *bash* shell; the hash mark (#) is the prompt for the *root* user.

---

**TIP**

Indicates a tip, suggestion, or general note.

---

---

**WARNING**

Indicates a warning or caution.

---

*Menu symbols*

> When looking at the menus for any application, you will see some symbols associated with keyboard shortcuts for a particular command. For example, to open a document in Microsoft Word, you could go to the File menu and select Open (File → Open), or you could issue the keyboard shortcut, ⌘-O.
>
> Figure 1 shows the symbols used in the various menus to denote a keyboard shortcut.

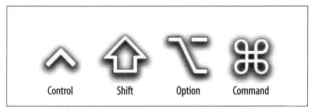

*Figure 1. Keyboard accelerators for issuing commands*

> Rarely will you see the Control symbol used as a menu command option; it's more often used in association with mouse clicks to emulate a right click on a two-button mouse or for working with the *bash* shell.

---

# PART I

# Mac OS X Survival Guide

This first part is intended to show those who are new to Mac OS X how to acclimate quickly to their new environment. For Windows and Unix users who are Switching to Mac OS X, most everything will be new, while users of older versions of Mac OS, such as Mac OS 8 or 9, will have to adjust the most to relearn the Mac.

This part of the book covers:

- Changes to Mac OS X from Mac OS 9
- Tips for "Switchers" coming to Mac OS X from Windows and Unix systems such as Linux or one of the BSDs (FreeBSD, NetBSD, or OpenBSD)

## Changes to Mac OS X from Mac OS 9

There are many noticeable changes in the user interface from earlier versions of the Mac OS to Mac OS X, while others may not be so apparent. Two of the biggest changes from Mac OS 9 to Mac OS X can be found in the Apple menu and the Control Panels.

### The Apple Menu

The Apple menu, displayed as an apple symbol (&#63743;) in the menu bar, is completely different; you can no longer store aliases for files, folders, or applications there. The following lists what you'll find in Mac OS X's Apple menu.

*About This Mac*

This option pops open a window that supplies you with information about your Mac. Aside from telling you that you're running Mac OS X on your computer, the window shows you which version of Mac OS X is installed, how much memory you have, and the speed and type of processor in your computer. Clicking on the More Info button launches the System Profiler (*/Applications/ Utilities*), which gives you a greater level of detail about your computer.

---

**TIP**

Clicking on the version number in the About This Mac window will reveal the build number of Mac OS X; clicking it again will show the hardware serial number for your computer. These small details are important to have when contacting Apple Customer Service and when reporting a probable bug.

---

In earlier versions of the Mac OS, the About box would change depending on which application was active. For information about the application, you now have to use the Application menu (located to the right of the Apple menu) and select the About option.

*Software Update*

This launches the Software Update preferences panel and checks for updates for Mac OS X and other Apple software installed on your system.

*Mac OS X Software*

This option takes you to Apple's Mac OS X page (*http:// www.apple.com/macosx/*) in your default web browser.

*System Preferences*

This launches the System Preferences application, which replaces most of the Control Panels from earlier versions of the Mac OS. See "System Preferences" later in this book for more details.

---

*Dock*

This menu offers a quick way to change settings for the Dock (described later).

*Location*

This is similar to the Location Manager Control Panel from earlier versions of the Mac OS: it allows you to change locations quickly for connecting to a network and/or the Internet.

*Recent Items*

This menu option combines the Recent Applications and Recent Documents options from Mac OS 9's Apple menu into one convenient menu. A Clear Menu option allows you to reset the recent items from the menu.

*Force Quit*

Thanks to Mac OS X's protected memory, you don't have to restart the entire system if an application crashes or freezes. Instead, you can come here (or use Option-⌘-Esc) to open a window that lists the applications running on your system. To Force Quit an application, simply click on the application name, then click on Force Quit.

Unlike applications, you cannot force quit the Finder by Control-clicking on its icon in the Dock. Instead, you need to restart it from here. When you select the Finder, the Force Quit button changes to Relaunch; click that button to restart the Finder.

*Sleep*

Selecting this option immediately puts your Mac into sleep mode. This is different from the settings you dictate in System Preferences → Energy Saver for auto-sleep functionality. To "wake" your computer from sleep mode, simply press any key.

If you close the lid (or display) on your iBook or Power-Book while it is running, the computer goes into sleep mode. Opening your laptop should wake up your system automatically; if it doesn't, try hitting the spacebar or the Return key.

*Restart*

> This restarts your Mac. If any applications are running, they will be automatically shut down, and you will be prompted to save changes for any files that were open.

*Shutdown*

> This shuts down your Mac. You can also shut down your Mac by pressing the Power-on button, which will open a dialog box with the options for restarting, shutting down, or putting your Mac to sleep.

*Log Out*

> This option logs you out of your system, taking you back to a login screen. The keyboard shortcut to log out is Shift-⌘-Q.

---

**TIP**

Sleep, Restart, Shutdown, and Log Out have moved from Mac OS 9's Special menu into Mac OS X's Apple menu. If you're looking for a menu option for Empty Trash, you will need to be in the Finder (Finder → Empty Trash, or Shift-⌘-Delete).

---

## Think System Preferences, Not Control Panels

One of the most notable changes in Mac OS X is that the Control Panels (⌘ → Control Panels) aren't in the Apple menu. The Control Panels of old are now replaced by System Preferences. Table 1 lists the Control Panels from Mac OS 9 and shows you their equivalents in Mac OS X.

*Table 1. Mac OS 9's Control Panels and their disposition in Mac OS X*

| Mac OS 9 Control Panel | Equivalent in Mac OS X |
| --- | --- |
| Appearance | System Preferences → Desktop & Screen Saver |
| | System Preferences → Appearance |
| Apple Menu Options | System Preferences → Appearance |

---

*Table 1. Mac OS 9's Control Panels and their disposition
in Mac OS X (continued)*

| Mac OS 9 Control Panel | Equivalent in Mac OS X |
| --- | --- |
| AppleTalk[a] | System Preferences → Network → AppleTalk |
| ColorSync | System Preferences → ColorSync |
| Control Strip[a] | Gone; replaced by Dock. |
| Date & Time | System Preferences → Date & Time |
| DialAssist[a] | System Preferences → Network → Show → Internal Modem |
| Energy Saver[a] | System Preferences → Energy Saver |
| Extensions Manager | Gone. With Mac OS X, you no longer need to manage your extensions. To view the extensions on your system, launch the Apple System Profiler (*/Applications/Utilities*) and click on the Extensions tab. |
| File Exchange[a] | Gone; use Bluetooth File Exchange (*/Applications/ Utilities*). |
| File Sharing | System Preferences → Sharing |
| File Synchronization | Gone. |
| General Controls | System Preferences → Appearance |
| Infrared[a] | System Preferences → Network → Show → infrared-port. |
| Internet | Gone. |
| Keyboard | System Preferences → Keyboard & Mouse<br>System Preferences → International → Input Menu |
| Keychain Access | Applications → Utilities → Keychain Access |
| Launcher | Gone; replaced by Dock. |
| Location Manager[a] | System Preferences → Network → Location (This applies only to network settings, unlike Location Manager.)<br> → Location |
| Memory[a] | Gone. |
| Modem[a] | System Preferences → Network → Show → Internal Modem |
| Monitors | System Preferences → Displays |
| Mouse[a] | System Preferences → Keyboard & Mouse |

*Table 1. Mac OS 9's Control Panels and their disposition in Mac OS X (continued)*

| Mac OS 9 Control Panel | Equivalent in Mac OS X |
| --- | --- |
| Multiple Users[a] | System Preferences → Accounts |
| Numbers | System Preferences → International → Formats → Numbers |
| Password Security | System Preferences → Security |
| QuickTime Settings | System Preferences → QuickTime |
| Remote Access[a] | Applications → Internet Connect |
| Software Update[a] | System Preferences → Software Update |
| Sound[a] | System Preferences → Sound |
| Speech | System Preferences → Speech |
| Startup Disk[a] | System Preferences → Startup Disk |
| TCP/IP[a] | System Preferences → Network |
| Text | System Preferences → International → Language |
| Trackpad[a] | System Preferences → Mouse |
| USB Printer Sharing | System Preferences → Sharing → Services → Printer Sharing |
| Web Sharing | System Preferences → Sharing → Services → Personal Web Sharing |

[a] Not supported under Classic.

See "System Preferences," later in this book, for additional information about each of the preference panels.

## Other Missing Items

Some other things you'll find missing from Mac OS X include:

*Apple CD Audio Player*
   This has been replaced by iTunes.

*The Chooser*
   To configure a printer in Mac OS X, you need to use the Print Center (*/Applications/Utilities*). To connect to a

server or another computer on your network, you need to use Go → Connect to Server (⌘-K). The Chooser still exists for printing and networking from the Classic environment (described later).

*Put Away (⌘-Y)*

This command had two functions: to eject a disk (floppy or CD), or to move an item out of the Trash back to its place of origin. Instead, ⌘-E can be used to eject a CD or unmount a networked drive.

---

**TIP**

On newer iBooks and PowerBooks, pressing the F12 key will eject a CD or DVD.

---

*Graphing Calculator*

Gone; no replacement.

*Note Pad and SimpleText*

These have been replaced by the much more versatile TextEdit application.

*Scrapbook*

The Scrapbook has gone to the scrap heap.

*SimpleSound*

This has been replaced by the Sound panel, which can be accessed from System Preferences → Sound → Sound Effects.

# Tips for Switchers

If you're one of the many people who have finally decided to make the "Switch" to Mac OS X from Windows or another Unix operating system (such as FreeBSD, Solaris, or Linux), this section is intended to be a quick reference guide to aid in your transition to the Mac. I've tried to point out some key differences between your old platform and Mac OS X to help you acclimate yourself with your Mac.

---

## General Tips for Switchers

The following tips apply (in general terms) to Switchers from both Windows and other Unix-based systems, as well as to users who've made the transition from Mac OS 9 to Mac OS X:

- The Mac user interface has only one menu bar—at the top of the screen—instead of one on each window. The menu bar's contents change depending on which application is currently active. The name of the application that's currently active appears in bold text next to the Apple menu.

- At first, you will sorely miss your two- or three-button mouse. You can emulate right-button functions by holding down the Control key when clicking. Mac OS X also supports multibutton mice, mapping the Control key to the right mouse button.

- If you have a scrollwheel mouse, Mac OS X should detect it automatically and provide options for how the scrollwheel performs via the System Preferences → Mouse preferences panel.

- To find which Mac OS X applications you have on your system, click on the Applications icon in the Finder's toolbar.

- To find out which Mac OS 9 applications you have on your system, click on Finder → Computer → Macintosh HD → Applications (Mac OS 9).

- Printer setup and queue control is handled by the Print Center application (*/Applications/Utilities*) or via System Preferences → Print & Fax → Printing → Set Up Printers. If you find that you need to configure printers or start and stop print queues often, you might want to consider adding Print Center to your Dock by dragging its icon there for easy access.

- Each user has his own desktop, which is stored in */Users/ username/Desktop*. By default, many documents (such as files downloaded from the Web or saved attachments) are stored in */Users/username/Documents*. Files stored in the Desktop folder will appear on the desktop when you log in.

- When you first get your Mac, you should run Software Update (System Preferences → Software Update, or  → Software Update) to make sure that your system and other Apple software is up-to-date. Once your system has been updated, set System Preferences to check for updates weekly.

- Looking for an update to some piece of non-Apple software you're running on your system? Check out Version Tracker (*http://www.versiontracker.com*).

If you're a Mac OS 9 user and you are on the fence about switching or upgrading to Mac OS X, now's the time to get off that fence and upgrade. Mac OS X is a more stable operating system than Mac OS 9, and you can still run most Mac OS 9 applications on top of Mac OS X with help from the Classic environment and without a performance hit.

## Tips for Windows Switchers

If you're coming to the Mac from a Windows system, these tips are for you:

- The Apple menu, located at the far left of the menu bar, is roughly analogous to the Windows Start menu (although it doesn't list common utilities).

- The basic GUI control program, akin to the Windows Explorer or the Window Manager in Windows, is called the Finder. Clicking on its icon in the Dock (the blue smiley-face icon) brings up a Finder window, not the desktop, as you might expect.

- System Preferences is analogous to the Windows Control Panel. The System Preferences application can be launched by clicking on its icon in the Dock (the one that looks like a light switch with a gray apple next to it).

- The Dock is analogous to the Windows Task Bar. It is initially populated with some frequently accessed applications, such as the Finder, System Preferences, and Sherlock. You can drag any program icon onto the Dock to create a shortcut to it that is accessible at all times.

- The Command key (⌘) provides many of the functions that you are used to having associated with the Control key. For example, use ⌘-C to copy, not Control-C; ⌘-S to save, not Control-S; etc.

- If you're accustomed to using Alt-Tab to switch between active applications, you should use ⌘-Tab to do the same thing on the Mac. (Even though the Option key does say "Alt" on it, the Option key doesn't do the same things that the Alt key does on a Windows system.)

- You can use StuffIt Expander (*/Applications/Utilities*) to unzip files by double-clicking on the Zip archive.

- You can zip up files from the command line in the Terminal application (*/Applications/Utilities*). See Part V for examples on how to zip and unzip files from the command line.

- If you really want Windows, you have the option to install Virtual PC (*http://www.microsoft.com/mac/products/virtualpc/virtualpc.aspx*), which allows you to run Windows applications on top of Mac OS X.

---

**TIP**

Windows users will benefit most from David Pogue's book, *Switching to the Mac: The Missing Manual*, copublished by Pogue Press and O'Reilly & Associates, Inc.

---

## Tips for Unix Switchers

If you're coming to Mac OS X from another Unix OS, these tips are for you:

- The Unix command line (the *bash* shell) is available via the Terminal application (*/Applications/Utilities*). If you plan to work frequently from the command line, you should add the Terminal application's icon to the Dock by dragging its icon there.

- The available user shells include *bash* (the default), *sh*, *tcsh*, *csh*, and *zsh*.

- All of your favorite scripting languages are available on Mac OS X, including sed, awk, Perl, Python, and Ruby. You'll also find development tools such as *bison*, *cvs*, *flex*, *gcc*, *gdb*, *imake*, *make*, and more.

- If you need the X Window System, Apple has optimized a version of XFree86 to run on top of Mac OS X. For more information about Apple's X11 implementation, go to *http://www.apple.com/macosx/x11*. If X11 is already installed, it can be found in */Applications/Utilities*.

- If your favorite Unix utility isn't available on Mac OS X, download and install Fink (*http://fink.sourceforge.net*). Fink uses Debian tools such as *dpkg* and *apt-get* to provide binary package management. A complete list of Fink packages can be found at *http://fink.sourceforge.net/list. php*; when installing from Fink, it also takes care of any package dependencies.

- While the Terminal application gives you a command-line interface, it is slightly different from an *xterm*. For example, the Terminal doesn't have a *.xinitrc* file from which to control how Terminal windows appear. Instead, use Terminal → Show Info (⌘-I) to configure your Terminal's appearance.

- Unix users and administrators will quickly find out that some of the standard admin commands are missing or that useful options aren't there. For example, the commands for managing users and groups don't exist—for that, you need to use the System Preferences panels and/or NetInfo Manager (*/Applications/Utilities*).

- To find out which Unix applications and utilities are available, you can poke around in */usr/bin*, */usr/local/bin*, */usr/sbin*, */usr/share*, and */usr/libexec*.

---

**TIP**

To quickly list all the binary executables on your system, use Esc-? (so, Esc-Shift-?) or Control-X-! (using Shift-1 to get the exclamation mark). There are nearly 1,000 command-line utilities on Mac OS X.

---

- By default, the *root* user (or *superuser*) isn't activated. If you are the only user on your system, you will have administrator privileges by default, which allows you to use the *sudo* command. See "The root User Account" later in this book for details on how to activate the *root* user.

---

**TIP**

For most tasks, the *sudo* command should suffice. Enable the *root* user account only if you must, taking into consideration the possible security risks that go along with a *root*-enabled system.

---

- You'll find lots of freeware applications and utilities for Mac OS X on SourceForge (*http://www.sourceforge.net*), as you have in the past for Linux and FreeBSD.
- If you're a Unix developer or system administrator, we suggest you pick up a copy of *Mac OS X Panther for Unix Geeks* (O'Reilly), which covers things such as the Terminal, Directory Services and NetInfo, compiling code with GCC, installing packages with Fink, and running the X Window System on top of Mac OS X.

---

# PART II

# Mac OS X Basics

This part of the book introduces you to the key features of Mac OS X's interface. Here we'll cover:

- Window Controls
- The Finder
- Keyboard Shortcuts
- The Dock
- Mac OS X and the Classic Environment
- Users and Logging In

## Window Controls

Windows in Mac OS X have an entirely different set of controls than those from earlier versions of the Mac OS. These window features are highlighted in Figure 2.

The controls are defined as follows:

1. Close window button (red)
2. Minimize window button (yellow)
3. Zoom, or maximize, window button (green)
4. Proxy icon
5. Filename
6. Toolbar button (not available on all windows)
7. Scrollbars and scroll arrows
8. Resize window control

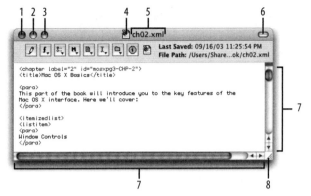

*Figure 2. Standard window controls in Mac OS X*

The top part of the window is known as the *titlebar*. The titlebar is home to the three colored window control buttons for closing (red), minimizing (yellow), and zooming (green) the window. Mousing over the buttons will change their state to be either an X, a minus sign (–), or a plus sign (+), respectively. These are visual cues to you as to the function the button performs.

With some applications, you'll notice that the red close window button has a dark-colored dot in its center. This means that the document you're working on has unsaved changes; if you save the document (File → Save, or ⌘-S), the dot will go away.

## Window Tips

The following are some tips for working with windows:

*Open a new window?*
　　File → Open (⌘-O).

*Close a window?*
　　File → Close (⌘-W).

*Close all open windows for an application?*
Option-click on the red close window button.

---

**TIP**

If there are changes that need to be saved in any of the windows being closed, you will be prompted to save the changes. Either hit Return to save the changes, or enter ⌘-D to invoke the Don't Save button.

A quick way to tell whether a window has unsaved changes is to look at the red close window button; if there is a dark red circle in its center, that means the document needs to be saved.

---

*Minimize a window?*
Click on the yellow minimize button.

Window → Minimize Window (⌘-M).

Double-click on the window's titlebar.

*Minimize all open windows for a single application?*
Option-⌘-M.

---

**TIP**

With some applications, Option-⌘-M might function differently. For example, issuing Option-⌘-M in Microsoft Word (Office v.X) will open the Paragraph format window (Format → Paragraph). Other applications that won't minimize all of the windows with this shortcut include the iChat AV, QuickTime Player, Terminal, and TextEdit. To be safe, you should save changes to the file before trying to minimize all the application's windows with Option-⌘-M.

---

*Quickly create an alias of an open file, or move it, depending on the app (e.g., Word)?*
Click and drag the file's proxy icon to a new location (i.e., the Desktop, Dock, Finder, etc.). The file must first be saved and named before an alias can be created.

Dragging a folder's proxy icon from a Finder window's titlebar moves that folder to the new location instead of creating an alias. If you want to create an alias for a folder, you should select the folder in the Finder, then Option-⌘-drag the folder to where you'd like the alias to be. As a visual cue to let you know you're creating an alias, the mouse pointer will change to a curved arrow.

*Find out where the file exists in the filesystem?*

Command-click on the proxy icon. This will pop open a context menu, showing you where the file exists. Selecting another item (such as a hard drive or a folder) from the proxy icon's context menu will open a Finder window taking you to that location.

*Hide the windows for other active applications?*

Option-⌘-click on the Dock icon for the application you're using, and the open windows for all other active applications will instantly hide. To bring another application's windows to the front, click on that application's Dock icon; to unhide all the other windows, select Show All from the application menu of the application you're currently using (e.g., Finder → Show All).

# The Finder

In earlier versions of the Mac OS, the Finder was located in the application menu at the far-right edge of the menu bar. The Finder was the application responsible for displaying the contents of a drive or folder; when double-clicked, a window would open, displaying either an Icon or List View of the contents. Mac OS X's Finder really isn't that different from Mac OS 9's Finder. It still displays the contents of drives and folders; however, the Finder is much more powerful and efficient, particularly in Panther.

The Finder serves as a graphical file manager, which offers three ways (or *Views*) to look at the files, folders, applications, and other filesystems (or *volumes*) mounted on your system. If you've used an earlier version of Mac OS X, you'll notice that Panther's Finder, shown in Figure 3, has changed dramatically.

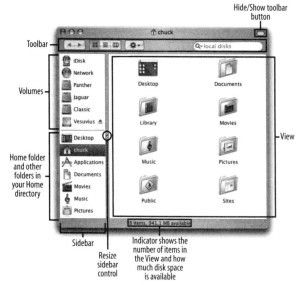

*Figure 3. Panther's new Finder and its controls*

Panther's Finder has three main sections:

Toolbar
    Located across the top of the Finder window, the toolbar offers buttons that let you go back or forward to a previous view, buttons for changing the three views (Icon, List, or Column), the new Action button, and a search field for quickly finding files and folders on your Mac.

*Sidebar*

Located on the left edge of the Finder window, the Sidebar offers a split view for accessing drives and other items on your Mac.

The top portion of the Sidebar has icons for any disks connected to your Mac. This includes hard drives and partitions, FireWire and USB drives, CDs and DVDs, iDisks, disk images, and networked drives such as FTP sites or Samba shares.

The bottom portion of the Sidebar includes clickable icons for getting at your Favorites, Desktop, and Home folder, as well as items found in the Applications, Documents, Movies, Music, and Pictures folders.

*The View*

This area of the Finder is the big section to the right of the Sidebar. The View displays the contents of the drives and folders of your system. The default View is Icon View, which displays the files and folders as named icons; however, you can change the view to either List or Column View by clicking on the appropriate button in the toolbar.

---

**TIP**

You can quickly change the Finder's viewpoint by using ⌘-1 for Icon View, ⌘-2 for List View, or ⌘-3 for Column View.

---

The toolbar's Action button is one of the marvels of the new Finder. If you click on a file or folder in the Finder and then click on the Action button (the one that looks like a little gear wheel), a pop-up menu appears, which lets you do any of the following:

- Create a new folder within the selected folder, or within the same folder if the item selected is a file.

- Open the Get Info window to see details about the selected item.

---

- Apply a color label (yes, labels are back in Panther) to the item.
- Duplicate the item.
- Create an alias of the item.
- Create a Zip archive of the selected file or folder. This is particularly handy when you want to quickly create a Zip archive of only a few files within a folder.

---

**TIP**

Command-click on the files you want to archive, then select Create Archive from the Action menu. To unzip an archive, select the Zip file and then select File → Open With → StuffIt Expander.

---

- Copy the selected item to the pasteboard. If an item has been copied to the pasteboard, a Paste option then becomes available in the Action item so you can paste a copy of the item in another location on your Mac.
- Show the available options for the View.

More later on the Finder's Toolbar, Sidebar, and how to search with the Finder; for now, let's look at the three Views available in the Finder:

*Icon View*

This shows the contents of a directory as either a file, folder, or application icon, as shown in Figure 4. Double-clicking on an icon will do one of three things: launch an application, open a file, or display the contents of a double-clicked folder in the Finder window.

Table 2 presents a list of keyboard shortcuts that can be used within the Finder's Icon View.

*Figure 4. The Finder in Icon View*

*Table 2. Icon View's keyboard shortcuts*

| Key command | Description |
| --- | --- |
| Up, Down, Left, and Right Arrow keys | Move through the icons in the View based on the key pressed. |
| Shift-Arrow key | When one icon is selected and the Shift-Arrow (Up, Down, Left, or Right) keys are pressed, the icon in that direction will be selected as well. |

*List View*

A directory's contents are displayed in a list, as shown in Figure 5. To display the contents of a folder, you can click on the disclosure triangle (the black triangle to the left of the folder), as illustrated in the figure.

Another way to navigate through the icons and folders in the Finder's List View is by using the keyboard, as noted in Table 3.

*Figure 5. The Finder in List View*

*Table 3. List View's keyboard shortcuts*

| Key command | Description |
|---|---|
| Down Arrow | Move down through the list of items. |
| Up Arrow | Move up through the list of items. |
| Right Arrow | Open a folder's disclosure triangle to reveal its contents. |
| Left Arrow | Close a folder's disclosure triangle to hide its contents. |
| Option-Right Arrow | Open a folder and any subfolders. |
| Option-Left Arrow | Close a folder and any subfolders. |

To open all the folders in the View, select all the View's contents (⌘-A) and use Option-Right Arrow (likewise, use Option-Left Arrow to close them again). To open all the folders in the View, including subfolders, add the Shift key (Shift-Option-Right Arrow to open, Shift-Option-Left Arrow to close).

*Column View*

Column View, shown in Figure 6, displays a directory's contents in column form. This is similar to List View, except that when you click on an item, a new pane opens to the right and either exposes the contents of a folder or displays some information (known as *metadata*) about a file, including its name, type, and file size.

*Figure 6. The Finder in Column View*

Table 4 lists the keyboard shortcuts that can be used within the Finder's Column View.

*Table 4. Column View's keyboard shortcuts*

| Key command | Description |
| --- | --- |
| Up, Down, Left, Right Arrow keys | Move through the columns in the View based on the key pressed |

The Finder's application menu has options for changing the Finder's preferences (Finder → Preferences) and for emptying the trash (Finder → Empty Trash, or Shift-⌘-Delete). New with Panther is a Secure Empty Trash option. If you select this item (Finder → Secure Empty Trash), the files in your Trash will be overwritten in such a way that they can't be recovered. When you use Secure Empty Trash, it takes a little longer for the Trash to empty as the system overwrites the files.

## The Finder's Toolbar

Along the top of the Finder window is a toolbar (shown in Figure 7), which offers a quick way to switch between the View modes mentioned earlier, or to search for files on your Mac.

You can add a file, folder, or application to the Finder toolbar by dragging and dropping its icon to the toolbar. Application icons that get added to the toolbar will launch with a single click, just as they do in the Dock.

### Hiding the toolbar

Located at the upper-right corner of the Finder window is an elliptical button that can be used to hide the Finder's toolbar, as shown in Figure 8.

In Panther, when you click on the Hide/Show toolbar button, the Finder's toolbar behaves differently than with earlier versions of Mac OS X. If you click on this button, the paned view goes away and the Finder takes on a remarkable likeness to the Finders that predate Panther. Clicking on the button again reverts the Finder to its normal self. If you are in Icon or List View with the toolbar hidden, the Finder window performs just like Mac OS 9's Finder windows. Double-clicking on a folder icon will open a new window for that folder, displaying its contents. Column View will function normally.

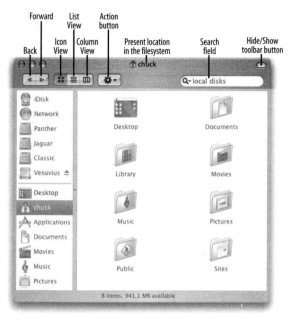

*Figure 7. The Finder toolbar*

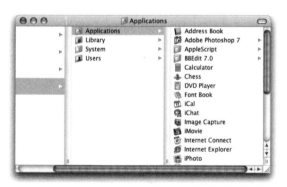

*Figure 8. The Finder window with a hidden toolbar*

## Customizing the toolbar

In addition to adding shortcuts to files, folders, and applications in the toolbar, you can also customize it in other ways. For example, if you don't like the current arrangement of buttons in the toolbar, you can ⌘-click on a button and drag it left or right. If you drag a button off the toolbar, it disappears with a poof.

Another way to customize the Finder's toolbar is to either select View → Customize Toolbar, or Option-⌘-click on the toolbar button. A sheet will flop out of the Finder's titlebar, revealing a host of other buttons you can add to the toolbar. To add a new button, just drag the item to the toolbar and place it where you'd like. When you've finished configuring the toolbar to your liking, click on the Done button.

# The Finder's Sidebar

As mentioned earlier, Panther's Finder has a Sidebar (shown in Figure 8). The Sidebar has the two panes located on the left side of the Finder window. The top-left pane displays any volumes that are mounted on your Mac, including your hard drive (and any of its partitions), FireWire and USB drives, disk images, your iDisk (if you have a .Mac account), and any network volumes you might be connected to, such as an AFP, NFS, or SMB drive.

The bottom-left pane of the Sidebar includes icons to quickly take you to other folders in your Home folder, including:

- Desktop
- The root level of your Home folder
- Applications
- Documents
- Movies
- Music
- Pictures

Volumes automatically appear in the upper portion of the Sidebar as they are mounted. To create a shortcut to a file, folder, or application, drag the item's icon to the lower portion of the Sidebar and drop it wherever you'd like. When you need to open that item (or launch the application), all you need to do is click once on the icon, just as if it were in your Dock.

To remove an item from the Sidebar, simply drag the icon away from the Finder window and let go of the mouse button; the icon will disappear with a poof.

## Searching from the Finder

As shown earlier in Figure 7, the Finder's toolbar sports a Search field, which was added to the Finder in Mac OS X 10.2 (Jaguar), replacing Sherlock's old system search functionality. The Search field in Panther has been enhanced to allow you to search in the following places:

- On any local disks mounted on your system, including external drives
- Within your Home folder
- Within a selected disk or folder
- Everywhere on the system, including all of the three previously mentioned locations

To change the location of the search, click on the magnifying glass at the left edge of the Search field, and then select the location where you'd like to conduct your search. Your choices of places where you can search include:

*Local disks*
> Searches through all of the disks attached to your Mac, including hard disks, CDs, DVDs, FireWire, and USB drives.

*Home*
> Searches for files located in your Home folder and any of the folders within, including the Desktop, Documents, Library, Movies, Music, Pictures, Public, and Sites folders.

---

*Selection*

Use this option if you've selected a folder or disk volume in the Finder and just want to search the contents of a folder or volume.

*Everywhere*

Selecting this option will force the Finder to search not only through your hard drive, but also through any other volume mounted on your system, including networked drives.

---

**TIP**

Use the Everywhere option sparingly for conducting your searches, because the search will look at every file, in every folder, and on every disk attached to your Mac, which could take a long time to finish and return its results.

---

To search for a file on your system, select where you'd like the search conducted, and then type a word in the Search field. As soon as you start typing what you'd like to search for, the Finder kicks into high gear and immediately returns its results.

Search results are displayed in a split Finder window, as shown in Figure 9. Note that the titlebar for the Search window displays the location searched; the titlebar in Figure 9 tells us that the search was conducted in my Home directory.

Clicking on one of the items in the search results in the upper pane displays its path in the lower pane. If a folder is part of the search results, simply click once on the folder to see its contents in the Finder window; double-clicking an application icon launches the application, and double-clicking a file opens the file in the appropriate application (and launches that application too, if it isn't already active).

You can also do a more advanced search by opening up the Find window (shown in Figure 10), by selecting File → Find (⌘-F).

---

*Figure 9. The Finder's search results window*

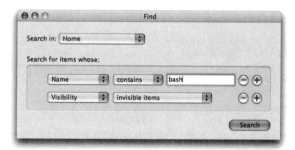

*Figure 10. The Finder's Find window*

The search shown in Figure 10 reveals any *bash* hidden files (i.e., files whose names begin with a period) in my Home directory. Clicking on the Search button will open a window, revealing the search results, which in this case will yield the *.bash_history* file.

# Finder Tips

The following are some tips for working with the Finder:

*Hide the Finder toolbar?*
> View → Hide Toolbar (Option-⌘-T).
>
> Click on the transparent button in the upper-right corner of the titlebar.

*Customize the Finder toolbar?*
> Finder → View → Customize Toolbar.
>
> Option-⌘-click the toolbar button.
>
> Control-click within the toolbar and select Customize Toolbar from the context menu.

*Show only the icons or text labels of items in the toolbar?*
> View → Customize Toolbar → Show; select Icon & Text from the pull-down menu.

*Speed up Finder searches?*
> Open the Finder's preferences panel (Finder → Preferences, or ⌘-,). Click on the Select button at the bottom of the window; this pops open a window that lets you select the languages to use when searching a file's contents. The fewer languages you select here, the faster your search will be.

*Locate a specific folder in the Finder?*
> Go → Go to Folder (or Shift-⌘-G).

---

### TIP

You can use Shift-⌘-G to go to directories such as */usr* and */bin*, which are part of Mac OS X's Unix filesystem.

---

*Search for hidden dot files on my system?*
> Open the Find dialog (File → Find, or ⌘-F). From the first pop-up menu, select Name, and in the field next to "contains," enter the word for which you'd like to search. In the next line, select Visibility from the pop-up menu and then select "invisible items" or "visible and invisible items" from the next pop-up menu.

---

# Keyboard Shortcuts

On the Mac (as with Windows and Linux desktops), you have two ways of invoking commands in the GUI: by using the menus or by issuing shortcuts for the commands on the keyboard. Not every menu item has a keyboard accelerator, but for the ones that do—the more common functions—using the keyboard shortcuts can save you a lot of time.

## Basic Keyboard Shortcuts

Table 5 lists the common key commands found in Mac OS X. While most of these commands function the same across all applications, the functions of some, such as ⌘-B and ⌘-I, can vary between programs, and others might work only when the Finder is active. For example, ⌘-B in Microsoft Word turns on boldface type or makes a selection bold, but in Xcode (formerly known as Project Builder), ⌘-B builds your application. Likewise, ⌘-I in Word italicizes a word or selection, but hitting ⌘-I after selecting a file, folder, or application on the desktop or in the Finder opens the Show Info window for the selected item.

*Table 5. Common keyboard shortcuts*

| Task | Key command |
|------|-------------|
| Open the Force Quit window | Option-⌘-Escape |
| Cycle forward through active applications | ⌘-Tab<br>⌘-Tab, Right Arrow |
| Cycle backward through active applications | Shift-⌘-Tab<br>⌘-Tab, Left Arrow |
| Cancel operation | ⌘-. |

*Table 5. Common keyboard shortcuts (continued)*

| Task | Key command |
| --- | --- |
| Open Mac Help | ⌘-? |
| Go back in the Finder view to the previous item | ⌘-[ |
| Go forward in the Finder view to the previous item | ⌘-] |
| Go to the folder that contains a selected item | ⌘-Up Arrow |
| Go to a folder in the Finder | Shift-⌘-G |
| Select all | ⌘-A |
| Hide/reveal the Finder's toolbar | Option-⌘-T |
| Copy | ⌘-C |
| Duplicate; creates a duplicate copy of a selected item. This command adds the word "copy" to the filename before the file extension. For example, if you were to select the file *file.txt* and hit ⌘-D, a new file named *file copy.txt* (with a space in the filename) would be created in the same directory as *file.txt*. | ⌘-D |
| Create an alias of a file | ⌘-L |
| Turn Dock hiding on/off | Option-⌘-D |
| Move item to Trash | ⌘-Delete |
| Empty Trash | Shift-⌘-Delete |
| Eject the selected disk image, CD, etc. | ⌘-E |
| Eject a CD or DVD | F12 |
| Find | ⌘-F |
| Hide application | ⌘-H |
| Get Info | ⌘-I |
| Show View options in the Finder | ⌘-J |
| Connect to Server | ⌘-K |
| Connect to a specific network | Shift-⌘-K |
| Minimize window | ⌘-M |
| Minimize all open windows for an application | Option-⌘-M |
| Open a new Finder window (This is a change from earlier versions of the Mac OS, where ⌘-N was used to create new folders.) | ⌘-N |
| Create new folder | Shift-⌘-N |

*Table 5. Common keyboard shortcuts (continued)*

| Task | Key command |
| --- | --- |
| Open file or folder; can also be used to launch applications | ⌘-O |
| Print file | ⌘-P |
| Quit application | ⌘-Q |
| Show original | ⌘-R |
| Paste | ⌘-V |
| Close window | ⌘-W |
| Close all open windows for an application | Option-⌘-W |
| Cut | ⌘-X |
| Undo | ⌘-Z |
| Redo (not available in all applications) | Shift-⌘-Z |
| Go to the Applications folder in the Finder | Shift-⌘-A |
| Go to the Utilities folder in the Finder | Shift-⌘-U |
| Go to Computer View in the Finder | Shift-⌘-C |
| Go to Home View in the Finder | Shift-⌘-H |
| Go to iDisk View in the Finder (requires a .Mac account) | Shift-⌘-I |
| Take a screenshot of the entire display | Shift-⌘-3 |
| Make and capture a rectangular selection of the display | Shift-⌘-4 |

## Startup and Shutdown Keys

For most users, starting and shutting down your Mac is fairly routine: press the Power-on button to start, and go to  → Shut Down to turn off the machine at night. But there are times when you need to do more, for whatever reason. Table 6 lists some of the additional keys you can use when starting, restarting, logging out, and shutting down your system.

---

**TIP**

Some of the keyboard shortcuts listed in Table 6 only work on newer hardware. If you are using an older Mac, these keyboard shortcuts might not work.

---

*Table 6. Keyboard shortcuts for starting, restarting, logging out, and shutting down*

| Key command | Description |
|---|---|
| C | Holding down the C key at startup boots from a CD (useful when installing or upgrading the system software). |
| N | Attempts to start up from a NetBoot server. |
| R | Resets the display for a PowerBook. |
| T | Holding down the T key at startup places your Mac into Target Mode as a mountable FireWire drive. After starting up, your screen will have a blue background with a floating yellow FireWire symbol. Target mode makes the hard drive(s) of your Mac appear as mounted FireWire drives when connected to another system. |
| | To exit Target mode, press the Power-on button to turn off your Mac. After your Mac has shut down completely, press the Power-on button again to restart normally. |
| X | Holding down the X key at startup forces the machine to boot into Mac OS X, even if Mac OS 9 is specified as the default startup disk. |
| ⌘-S | Boots into single-user mode. |
| ⌘-V | Boots into verbose mode, displaying all the startup messages onscreen. (Linux users will be familiar with this.) |
| Shift | Holding down the Shift key at startup invokes Safe Boot mode, turning off any unnecessary kernel extensions (*kexts*) and ignoring anything you've set in the Login Items preferences panel. |
| Option | Holding down the Option key at startup opens the Startup Manager, which allows you to select which OS to boot into. |
| Mouse button | Holding down the mouse button at startup ejects any disk (CD, DVD, or other removable media) that might still be in the drive. |
| Shift-Option-⌘-Q<br>Option + <img> → Log Out | Logs you off without prompting you first. |
| Option-Power-On<br>Option + <img> → Shut Down | Shuts down your system without prompting you first. |
| Option + <img> → Restart | Restarts your machine without prompting you first. |

| Key command | Description |
| --- | --- |
| Control-⌘-Power-On button | Forces an automatic shutdown of your system; this should be used only as a last resort, because it could mess up your filesystem.[a] |
| Control-Eject (F12) | Opens a dialog box that contains options for Restart, Sleep, and Shutdown. |

[a] Mostly, you'll just wait forever at the gray Apple startup screen while an *fsck* happens in the background.

# The Dock

One way to think about the Dock is as part Finder, part Apple menu, and part Launcher from earlier versions of the Mac OS. The Dock, shown in Figure 11, holds application aliases, making it easy for you to launch a program quickly with a single mouse click. To launch an application in the Dock, simply click on its icon. While the application is starting, its icon will "bounce" in the Dock; afterward, a black triangle will appear below the icon to indicate that the application is active.

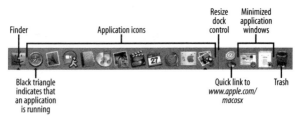

*Figure 11. The Dock*

By default, the Dock includes icons for the Finder, Safari, Mail, iChat AV, Address Book, iTunes, iPhoto, iMovie, iCal, QuickTime, System Preferences, and the Trash. To the left of the Trash icon is a quick link icon to Apple's Mac OS X web

---

site; clicking this icon will launch your default web browser and take you to Apple's web site.

---

---

To add an application icon to the Dock, simply drag its icon from the Finder to any location in the Dock and let go. To remove an application, click on the icon and drag it away from the Dock; the icon will disappear in a puff of smoke.

## Using and Configuring the Dock

Here are some helpful hints and tips for using and configuring your Dock:

*Quickly resize the Dock without launching its System Preferences panel?*
  Place the mouse over the divider bar in the Dock; the pointer changes from an arrow to a horizontal bar with arrows pointing up and down. Click on the divider bar and move the mouse up or down to make the Dock larger or smaller, respectively.

*Change the Dock's preferences?*
  &#63743; → Dock → Dock Preferences.

  System Preferences → Dock.

  Control-click on the Dock's divider bar and select Dock Preferences from the context menu.

*Add a program to the Dock?*
  Drag and drop an application's icon in the Dock from a Finder window.

---

After launching an application that isn't normally in the Dock, Control-click on that application's icon and select "Keep in Dock" from the pop-up menu.

*Remove a program from the Dock?*

Drag the application icon from the Dock and drop it anywhere.

*Change the Dock's location from the bottom of the screen to the left or right side?*

System Preferences → Dock → Position on screen.

 → Dock → Position on (Left, Bottom, or Right).

Control-click on the Dock's divider and select Position on screen → (Left, Bottom, or Right).

*Control the magnification of icons in the Dock?*

System Preferences → Dock → Magnification.

 → Dock → Turn Magnification (On/Off).

Control-click the Dock's divider and select Turn Magnification (On/Off).

*Make it so the Dock hides when I'm not using it?*

Option-⌘-D.

System Preferences → Dock → Automatically hide and show the Dock.

 → Dock → Turn Hiding (On/Off).

Control-click the Dock's divider and select Turn Hiding (On/Off).

*Stop application icons from bouncing when a program is launched?*

Go to System Preferences → Dock, and uncheck the checkbox next to "Animate opening applications." Instead of the application's icon bouncing, the disclosure triangle next to the icon will pulse until the program is fully launched.

# Dock Tricks

The following key-mouse commands can be used when clicking on an icon in the Dock:

*Command-click*

> If you ⌘-click an application icon in the Dock (or just click and hold down the mouse button), the Finder will open, taking you to that application's folder.

*Shift-⌘-click*

> Opens a Finder window to the application's location in the filesystem. This is similar to Control-clicking a Dock icon and selecting Show In Finder from its context menu.

*Control-click*

> If you Control-click a running application in the Dock (or click and hold down the mouse button), a pop-up menu will open, listing the windows that the application has open, as well as options to show the application in the Finder and to Quit the application.

> If you press the Option key while Control-clicking an icon in the Dock, the Quit option will toggle to Force Quit. This will not work for Classic applications (i.e., it works only for native Mac OS X applications).

*Option-click*

> Option-clicking has the same effect as Control-clicking, with one exception: Quit has been replaced by Force Quit in the pop-up menu.

*Option-⌘-click*

> Hides the windows of all other open applications and switches (if necessary) to the clicked application; similar to selecting Hide Others from an the application menu.

*Command-Tab*

> The ⌘-Tab function allows you to cycle through and switch between running applications quickly. As you press ⌘-Tab, the icons for running applications will highlight; when you release the ⌘ key, you will be taken to that application.

*Shift-⌘-Tab*

Shift-⌘-Tab has the reverse effect of ⌘-Tab; it moves backward through running applications in the Dock.

---

**TIP**

If you choose Empty Trash from the Dock by clicking on the icon and holding down the mouse button, the Trash icon's pop-up menu will empty locked files as well.

---

# Exposé

If you've ever wished for a quick way to get at your desktop or just the windows for a single application, Exposé is your answer. New to Panther, Exposé (shown in Figure 12) uses Quartz Extreme and OpenGL to make accessing windows—and your desktop—a dream come true.

*Figure 12. Exposé in action*

Exposé runs in the background and is configurable through its System Preferences panel (System Preferences → Exposé). The keyboard shortcuts for Exposé are listed in Table 7.

*Table 7. Keyboard shortcuts for Exposé*

| Key command | Description |
| --- | --- |
| F9 | Spreads out all open windows so they're viewable on the desktop |
| F10 | Separates just the application windows (not including the Finder windows) so they're viewable on the desktop |
| F11 | Clears all of the windows away from the desktop so you can see what's there |

After using one of Exposé's keyboard shortcuts, you can either click on the window you'd like to bring forward, or use the arrow keys on your keyboard to move around; to select a window, hit the Return key.

Using Exposé's preferences panel, you can configure Hot Corners for performing the actions of the function keys, or change the key settings to some other key combination.

# Mac OS X and the Classic Environment

To help bridge the application gap between Mac OS 9 and Mac OS X, Apple has built a *virtual machine* that enables you to run older Mac software under Mac OS X in what's known as *Classic*. Classic (or the "Classic environment") looks and feels just like Mac OS 9. The only exception is that the applications that run in Classic don't benefit from the features of Mac OS X, such as protected memory and advanced printing capability. Additionally, some Control Panels (⌘ → Control Panels), such as Control Strip, Memory, and Remote Access, are disabled. However, if you boot into Mac OS 9 instead of Mac OS X, you will be using a full version of the OS. See later for details on how to choose your Startup Disk. Basically, when you're running Classic, you are running a slightly watered-down version of Mac OS 9 *on top of* Mac OS X with only a minor performance hit.

Until all Mac applications are compliant with Mac OS X, you will also need to install a version of Mac OS 9 (9.2.2, to be exact). During the installation process, you can install both Mac OS 9 and Mac OS X on the same partition (or hard drive), or you can use Disk Utility (Installer → Open Disk Utility) to create a separate partition for each. Basically, you're creating a *dual-boot system*, which means you can boot your Mac into either OS. However, if you don't plan to run Classic applications, you won't need to install Mac OS 9.

---

**TIP**

Apple no longer ships or installs Mac OS 9 with Mac OS X or hardware. If you need a copy of Mac OS 9, use Sherlock to see if you can find a copy for sale on eBay.

---

The biggest benefit of installing Mac OS 9 and Mac OS X on separate partitions is being able to choose a startup volume at bootup by holding down the Option key. Otherwise, you can choose which OS to boot using the Startup Disk Control Panel (Mac OS 9) or System Preferences → Startup Disk (Mac OS X).

---

**TIP**

If you use the Activity Monitor (*/Applications/Utilities*) or the *top* command, described later, look for a process named *TruBlueEnvironment*. This is the Classic process—and all the applications running under Classic—in action.

---

To launch a Classic application, locate the application using the Finder (Finder → Macintosh HD → Applications (Mac OS 9)), and double-click on the application icon. The Classic environment will start if it isn't already running.

If you frequently use a particular Classic application, you can also add it to the Dock by dragging its icon to any location in the Dock. However, Control-clicking a Classic application's icon will not reveal a Dock menu; this support is provided only to native Mac OS X applications that use Carbon or Cocoa.

New to Panther, you can now add a menulet for Classic to the menu bar. To enable this menu, open the Classic preferences panel, and go to the Start/Stop pane. Click on the checkbox next to "Show Classic status in menu bar," and the menulet appears as anticipated. From this menu, you can start and stop Classic, and even access items in Mac OS 9's Apple menu. For people who rely on Classic a lot, this is a great new feature, since most Mac OS 9 users tend to place aliases for frequently used applications in the Apple menu.

While it's easy to use a Classic application on files saved on your Mac OS X partition, you will have a hard time accessing files saved on non-AFP networked drives. For example, if you're running Office 2001 and you want to open a Word document (*filename.doc*) on the partition named *Maui*, you won't find that drive in Word 2001's Open dialog. Fortunately, you can use the Terminal application to launch Word 2001 *and* open the file in one fell swoop. To do this, launch the Terminal application (*/Applications/Utilities*) and issue the following command on the command line:

```
open /Volumes/Maui/filename.doc
```

This command instructs your computer to open *filename.doc* (found on */Volumes/Maui*) using Microsoft Word. For more information about how to use the Terminal application, see "Configuring and Using the Terminal" later in this book.

## Users and Logging In

When you first install Mac OS X (or when you first boot your new hardware), you have to create at least one user account. Mac OS 9 first introduced the option of setting up a multiuser Mac system, but you weren't required to set up individual user accounts as with Mac OS X.

## Tips for Users

Here are some helpful hints to assist you in managing your user account:

*Configuring my login?*
> System Preferences → Accounts → Login Options.

*Change my login password?*
> System Preferences → Accounts → *username* → Password.
>
> Use the *passwd* command in the Terminal.

---

**TIP**

When choosing a password, you should avoid using dictionary words (i.e., common, everyday words found in the dictionary) or something that could be easily guessed. To improve your security, choose an alphanumeric password. Remember, passwords are case-sensitive, so you can mix upper- and lowercase letters in your password as well.

---

*Add another user to the system?*
> System Preferences → Accounts → click on the plus sign (+) below the Login Options button (requires administrator privileges).

---

**TIP**

Unix administrators might be tempted to use the *useradd*, *userdel*, and *usermod* commands to add, remove, and modify a user, respectively, from the Terminal. The only problem is, *you can't*; those commands don't exist on Mac OS X.

---

*Remove a user from the system?*

System Preferences → Accounts → *username* → click on the minus sign (–) below the Login Options button (requires administrator privileges). After a user has been deleted, that user's directories (and everything within) is packaged up in a disk image (as *username.dmg*) and placed in the */Users/Deleted Users* folder. This disk image can be deleted only by someone with administrator privileges.

---

### TIP

When you're logged in, you can't remove yourself from the system. If you want to remove your user account from the system, you have to log out and log back in as another user.

---

*Give a user administrator privileges?*

System Preferences → Accounts → *username* → Security → Allow user to administer this computer (requires administrator privileges).

*Restrict which applications a user can use?*

System Preferences → Accounts → *username* → Limitations (this pane is grayed out if the user has administrator privileges). The Limitations pane gives you three options:

*No limits*

The user has no restrictions on the type of applications he can use; he just can't administer the system. This is the default option for nonadministrative users.

*Some Limits*

This section lets you specify some things the user can do, such as burn CDs and DVDs, or change his password and restrict which applications he can use. By default, users who have Some Limits are restricted from using any of the Utilities (*/Applications/ Utilities*).

---

*Simple Finder*

> This is the most restrictive option you can apply to a user. This keeps the user from using the System Preferences for anything and gives him few options from his Dock.

---

**TIP**

Keep the Simple Finder in mind if you have a user you'd like to restrict from issuing Unix commands. You can cut off a user's access to the Terminal application by clicking the disclosure triangle next to Utilities and then unchecking the box next to the Terminal.

---

*Keep a user from changing her password?*

> System Preferences → Accounts → *username* → Limitations → uncheck the box next to Change password.

*Turn off automatic login?*

> System Preferences → Accounts → *username* → Login Options → uncheck the box next to "Log in automatically as *username*."

*Allow a user to log in to my Mac from a Windows system?*

> System Preferences → Sharing → Services; check the box next to Windows Sharing.

*Turn on Fast-User switching?*

> System Preferences → Accounts → *username* → Login Options → click on the checkboxes next to "Automatically log in as..." and "Enable fast user switching."

*Set a password hint?*

> The easy way to do this is by going to System Preferences → Accounts → *username* → Password pane. When you click in the Password Hint box, a sheet slides down from the titlebar, asking you for your password; enter your password and hit Return. Now, select the text in the Password Hint field, type in a new hint, and hit Return to save the change.

---

Now for the (sort of) hard way. You can also use NetInfo Manager (*/Applications/Utilities*) to change your password hint. You need to have administrator privileges to perform these steps:

1. Launch NetInfo Manager (*/Applications/Utilities*).

2. Click on the lock at the lower-left corner of the window and enter the admin user's password.

3. In the columns at the top half of the window, select users → *username* (e.g., users → chuck).

4. In the lower-half of the window, click on the hint line in the Property column, then double-click in the Value(s) column.

5. Type in a login hint, and hit Return to accept the value.

6. Click on the lock in the lower-left corner of the window to prevent any further changes from being made. When you click on the lock, an alert window will appear; click on the "Update this copy" button to accept the changed login hint.

7. Quit NetInfo Manager.

*Find out which users have admin privileges?*

System Preferences → Accounts. Users with administrator privileges will have Admin listed next to their names in the Type column.

Launch NetInfo Manager (*/Applications/Utilities*). In the Directory Browser pane, select / → groups → admin. In the lower half of the window, look at the Property value next to users; you'll see something like (root, *username*) in the Value(s) column. (Requires administrator privileges.)

*Add a new group?*

Launch NetInfo Manager (*/Applications/Utilities*). In the Directory Browser pane, select / → groups. From the menu bar, go to Directory → New Subdirectory (⌘-N). (Requires administrator privileges.)

In the Directory pane below, select the *new_directory* name by double-clicking on it, type in a new group name (e.g., *editorial*), and then click again on *new_directory* in the Directory Browser pane. A warning message will appear, asking you if you want to save the changes (click Save). Another message window will appear, asking you to confirm the modification; click on the "Update this copy" button, and the new group name will be applied in the Directory Browser pane.

---

### TIP

As with the user-related Unix commands, Unix users will notice that the various group commands (*groupadd*, *groupdel*, *groupmod*, *gpasswd*, *grpconv*, and *grpunconv*) are missing from Mac OS X. You will need to use Net-Info Manager (*/Applications/Utilities*) to manage groups.

---

If your system has more than one user on it, a Shared directory will be created in the Users folder. Because users are allowed to add or modify files only within their own home directories, this is a place where you can place items to be shared with the other users.

## User Subdirectories

Once created, each user is provided with a series of subdirectories in his Home directory (*/Users/username*). These directories, listed here, can be used for storing anything the user desires, although some have specific purposes:

*Desktop*
　　This directory contains the items found on your desktop, including any files, folders, or application aliases you've placed there.

*Documents*
　　While it isn't mandatory, the Documents directory can be used as a repository for any files or folders you create. Most applications will save files here by default.

---

*Library*

This directory is similar to the */System/Preferences* directory found in earlier versions of the Mac OS; it contains resources used by applications, but not the applications themselves.

*Movies*

This is a place where you can store movies you create with iMovie, or where you can hold QuickTime movies you create or download from the Internet.

*Music*

This directory can be used to store music and sound files, including *.aiff*, *.mp3*, etc. This is also where the iTunes Library is located.

*Pictures*

This directory can be used as a place to store photos and other images. iPhoto also uses the Pictures directory to house its iPhoto Library directory, which contains the photo albums you create.

*Public*

If you enable file or web sharing (System Preferences → Sharing), this is where you can place items you wish to share with other users. Users who access your Public directory can see and copy items from this directory.

Also located within the Public folder is the Drop Box folder. If you enable File Sharing (System Preferences → Sharing → Services → File Sharing), this is where other users can place files after connecting to your Mac.

*Sites*

If you enable Personal Web Sharing (System Preferences → Sharing → Services), this is the directory that will house the web site for your user account.

## The root User Account

On any Unix system, the *root* user has the authority to issue any command, giving that user extreme power. Because of the risks associated with that power (such as the ability to permanently delete the entire filesystem), the *root* user account has been disabled by default on Mac OS X. However, there are two ways you can enable the *root* user account: by using NetInfo Manager or from the command line. In both cases, you must already have administrator privileges on the system.

---

**TIP**

If you're the only user on the system, you will have administrator privileges by default. As such, if there is a particular function or command that can be issued only by the *root* user, you should use the *sudo* command.

---

Follow these steps to enable the *root* user account from NetInfo Manager:

1. Launch NetInfo Manager (*/Applications/Utilities*).

2. To make changes to the NetInfo settings, click on the padlock in the lower-left corner of the NetInfo window. You will be asked for the administrator's name and password; enter those, and click OK.

3. In the menu bar, select Security → Enable Root User.

4. You will be asked to enter a password for the *root* user. In earlier versions of Mac OS X, the *root* password had to be eight characters or less; however, in Panther, the *root* password must only be more than five characters in length. Click OK, and then enter the password again to confirm the password for the *root* user account. Click on the Verify button to confirm the password and enable the *root* account.

5. If you have no further changes to make in NetInfo Manager, click on the padlock at the lower-left of the window to prevent further changes from being made, and quit the application (⌘-Q).

---

To enable the *root* user account using the Terminal, enter the following command:

```
[MacPanther:~] chuck$ sudo passwd root
Password: *******
Changing password for root.
New password: ********
Retype new password: ********
[MacPanther:~] chuck$
```

The first time you're asked for a password, enter your own. Once you're verified by the system to have administrator privileges, you will be asked to enter and confirm a new password for the *root* user account.

---

### TIP

The asterisks shown in this example won't appear onscreen when you enter the passwords; actually, nothing will happen onscreen. If you make a mistake while entering the password, you can always hit the Backspace or Delete key to go back over what you typed; then just re-enter the password.

---

Once the *root* account has been assigned a password, you can use it to log in with the username *root*.

If you find that you need to access a directory or issue a command that requires *root* (or *superuser*) privileges, you can temporarily log in as the *root* user by issuing the *su* command:

```
[MacPanther:~] chuck$ su
Password: ********
[MacPanther:/Users/chuck] chuck#
```

Notice how the prompt has changed from chuck$ to chuck#. The # prompt is an indicator that you are running as *root*. As *root*, you should be careful about what you type.

After you've finished your business as *root*, type *exit*, and hit Return to log out as the *root* user and return to your normal user prompt.

## Get Info and Setting File Permissions

Get Info gives you access to all sorts of information about the files, directories, and applications on your system. To view the information for an item, click on its icon in the Finder, and either go to File → Get Info or use its keyboard shortcut, ⌘-I. The Get Info window has six different panes, which offer different kinds of information about the file. To reveal the content of one of these items, click on its disclosure triangle to expand the pane. The panes of the Get Info window include the following:

*General*

This tells you the basics about the file, including its kind, size, where it's located in the filesystem, and when it was created and last modified. If you are looking at the Info for a file, you will see two checkboxes in the General section: Stationary Pad and Locked. If you enable these options, the file can be used as a template or read-only, respectively.

*Name & Extension*

This displays a text box with the name of the file or directory.

*Content index*

This pane is available only when you use Get Info on a folder or directory (not with individual files); it tells you whether the contents of a folder have been indexed. Indexing stores information about the files contained within that directory in an information database used by the Find command when searching for files on your system. To index a folder, click on the Index Now button; this might take some time, depending on how many files or folders are contained within the folder.

*Open with Application*

This option is available only if you select a file (i.e., not a folder or an application). Here you can specify which application will open this file or all similar files.

*Preview*

Depending on the file type, you can view the contents of the file here (this also works for playing sounds and QuickTime movies).

*Ownership & Permissions*

This displays the name of the owner and the name of the group to which the file belongs. It also allows you to set access privileges to that file for the Owner, Group, and Others on the system.

*Comments*

This field can contain some basic information about the file, folder, or application.

The Get Info window for applications has the General Information, Name & Extension, and Ownership & Permissions options mentioned previously (although the Ownership & Permissions options are disabled by default), as well as one or both of the following options:

*Languages*

Shows the languages supported by the application. The languages are displayed with checkboxes next to them. To make an application run faster, turn off the languages you don't need by unchecking the box.

*Plug-ins*

If applicable, this lists the available plug-ins for the application. For example, iMovie and iPhoto's Info windows have a Plug-ins section.

Noticeably missing from a Mac OS X application's Get Info window is the Memory option. Because memory for applications is assigned dynamically by virtual memory, you no longer have to specify how much memory an application requires. However, if you use Get Info on a Mac OS 9 application, the Memory option will be there.

# PART III

# System Tools

This part introduces you to the various tools that accompany Mac OS X. The sections in this part are intended to provide an overview of the following:

- System Preferences
- Applications and Utilities
- Xcode Tools

Part V provides additional information about how to use and apply the System Preferences for configuring your system, as well as specific uses for some of Mac OS X's standard Applications and Utilities.

## System Preferences

As mentioned earlier, Mac OS X's System Preferences perform many of the same functions as Mac OS 9's Control Panels. To launch the System Preferences application, simply click on the light-switch icon in the Dock, and the window shown in Figure 13 appears.

As you'll notice, the System Preferences are broken down into four categories: Personal, Hardware, Internet & Network, and System. There is also a customizable toolbar at the top of the window, similar to the toolbar in the Finder window. If you find yourself using a particular System Preference often, drag its icon to the toolbar. Likewise, if there is one you use rarely, or can add a menu item for (such as the

*Figure 13. The System Preferences window*

Displays panel), drag the icon away, and the item will be removed from the toolbar.

Unlike the Finder's toolbar, you cannot customize the System Preferences toolbar. (You can customize the Finder's toolbar by Control-clicking on the toolbar itself and selecting Customize Toolbar from the context menu.) Thankfully, not all hope is lost, though. You can add and remove icons from the System Preferences toolbar by dragging an icon onto or off the toolbar. When you drag an icon off the toolbar, the icon disappears in a puff of smoke, similar to what happens when you remove an icon from the Dock.

---

**TIP**

If you Shift-click on the Toolbar button, System Preferences' toolbar will hide and reveal itself slowly. You won't gain anything by this, but it's kind of fun to do once or twice.

---

You can also change the size of the icon and the text labels for the icons by ⌘-clicking on the toolbar button as follows:

- The first time you ⌘-click reduces the size of toolbar icons and the text labels.
- The second time you ⌘-click removes the text labels and displays the icons at the normal size.
- The third time you ⌘-click reduces the size of the toolbar icons without the text labels.
- The fourth time you ⌘-click removes the panel icons and replaces them with large text labels.
- The fifth time you ⌘-click reduces the size of the text labels without the panel icons.
- The sixth time you ⌘-click returns the icons and text labels for the panels in the toolbar to their normal, original size.

---

**TIP**

This also works in applications such as Mail and the Omni applications (such as OmniWeb, OmniGraffle, and OmniOutliner). If you add the Shift key to any of these ⌘-click combinations (i.e., Shift-⌘-click), you'll go backward through the cycle to the previous setting.

---

You can move the icons in the toolbar around by click-dragging them to a different position. The only icon you can't remove from the toolbar is the Show All icon, which is permanently fixed to the far left of the toolbar. Additionally, you can't place anything to the left of the divider bar in the toolbar.

When you click on one of the icons, the window changes to reflect that particular panel's settings, but the toolbar remains in place. To hide the toolbar, click on the transparent button in the upper-right corner of the window. To go back to the main view, click the Show All button (View → Show All Preferences, or ⌘-L). You can also select View →

Organize Alphabetically; this menu option changes the view of the System Preferences window to that shown in Figure 14.

*Figure 14. The System Preferences, listed alphabetically*

When you've completed setting your Mac's preferences, you can quit System Preferences by selecting System Preferences → Quit (⌘-Q), or by simply closing the System Preferences window, using Window → Close (⌘-W).

The next four sections provide an overview of the controls found in the System Preferences. For additional information on how to use the System Preferences panels to configure your system, see Part V.

---

**TIP**

Some of the System Preferences panels require administrator privileges. If you attempt to change a setting and are asked for a password, try using the password you used to log in to the computer. If that doesn't work, contact your system administrator for assistance.

---

# Personal

These items control the general look and feel of the Aqua interface:

*Appearance*

This panel, which used to be the General panel in Jaguar, specifies the colors used for buttons and menu items when selected, location of scrollbar arrows (top and bottom, or together, known as "Smart Scrolling" in Mac OS 9), and how a click in the scrollbar will be interpreted (scroll down one page or scroll to that location in the document). Here, you can specify the number of recent items to be remembered and listed in the  → Recent Items menu for Applications and Documents, as well as determine which font-smoothing style and size is best for your type of display.

*Desktop & Screen Saver*

This panel combines the Desktop and Screen Effects panels from Jaguar. It has two panes that you can use to set the background image for your desktop and to select your screen saver. The Desktop pane lets you choose the pattern, image, or color of your desktop. If you click on the checkbox next to Change picture at the bottom of the window, the desktop picture will change automatically based on the timing you select in the pull-down menu.

The Screen Saver pane lets you select one of Mac OS X's default screen saver modules. Here, you can set the amount of time your system must be inactive before the screen saver kicks in, require a password to turn off the screen saver, and specify Hot Corners for enabling/disabling the screen saver.

If you have a .Mac account, you can also choose from the .Mac Screen Effects or subscribe to another .Mac member's public slide show. To do this, click on the Configure button and enter the members' name (for example, *chuckdude*).

*Dock*

This is one of the ways you can configure your Dock (another is by going to  → Dock → Dock Preferences). See "Using and Configuring the Dock," earlier in this book, for details on the Dock.

*Exposé*

Exposé, as mentioned earlier, allows you to quickly gain access to any open window or to see what's on your desktop. For more information on using Exposé, see "Exposé" in Part II.

*International*

This is used to set the languages supported by your system. The language you specify during the installation process will be the default. Also found here are controls used to format the date, time, numbers, and currency, as well as the keyboard layout to be used for a country and its language.

If you select more than one language in the tabbed Input Menu pane, a menulet will appear in the menu bar, showing the flags for the countries whose languages will be supported on your system.

---

**TIP**

If you have your Mac configured to use more than one keyboard type, you can toggle between them using ⌘-Spacebar.

---

*Security*

The Security panel, new to Panther, let's you set up a FileVault for your Home folder by encrypting its contents. FileVault uses Kerberos authentication to encrypt and decrypt files automatically. To enable FileVault, you'll first need to set the master password, and then click on the Turn on FileVault button. After entering your login password (not the master password you've just set), you can turn on FileVault protection. All of the files in your Home folder will be encrypted with your login password. This protects your files from being accessed by other users on your computer, or from someone who might boot your Mac into Target Mode with malicious intent. When FileVault finishes encrypting your files, you will be required to log back in, after which you'll notice that the icon for your Home folder in the Finder has changed from a friendly looking house to an imposing metallic house that looks like a safe.

This panel also has checkboxes at the bottom, with options for requiring a password when waking your computer from sleep or screen saver mode, as well as for disabling automatic login and logging out automatically if your Mac has been inactive for a certain amount of time.

## Hardware

These panels are used to control the settings for the devices connected to your computer.

*Bluetooth*

This panel allows you to configure the settings for using Bluetooth to exchange files with other users and to synchronize data between your computer and other devices, such as cellular phones and PDAs. This item appears only if you have a Bluetooth-enabled PowerBook or a Bluetooth dongle (such as the one Apple promotes from D-Link) inserted into one of the USB slots.

*CDs & DVDs*

The items in the CDs & DVDs panel all share the same basic interface: a pull-down menu that lets you choose what the Mac does when it mounts various kinds of disks. You can choose to have it simply open the new media volume as a Finder window, launch an appropriate application (such as iTunes for music CDs and Disk Copy for blank discs), run a script, or prompt you for some other action to take.

---

*Displays*

This panel lets you set your monitor's resolution and its color-depth (256, thousands, or millions of colors). There is also an option to include a monitor menulet in the menu bar, as well as a slider control to set your monitor's brightness. If you have more than one monitor connected to your system, clicking on the Detect Displays button will allow you to specify settings for each display.

*Energy Saver*

This panel is used to set the auto-sleep settings for your computer. Here, you can specify the amount of time your system must be idle before putting your monitor, hard drive, or the entire system to sleep.

PowerBook and iBook users will also see two pull-down menus at the top of this panel. The first, Optimize Energy Settings, lets you select from one of four preset options or specify custom settings. The second pull-down menu, Settings for, gives you options for controlling the Energy Saver settings for when you're plugged in (Power Adapter) or when you're operating on battery (Battery Power).

*Ink*

This item appears only if you have a graphics tablet (such as a Wacom tablet) connected to your system. Ink controls how handwritten text is handled by the InkPad. The Gestures tab includes pen strokes for invoking commands such as Undo, Cut, Copy, Paste, inserting a space or carriage return (Vertical Space), and more.

*Keyboard & Mouse*

This panel combines the Keyboard and Mouse panels from Jaguar. There are four panes within the Keyboard & Mouse panel:

*Keyboard*

This pane controls the repeat rate when you depress a key and hold it down. You can specify the speed of the repeat (from slow to fast) and the delay between the time the key is first depressed until the repeat option kicks in (from long to short). If you select the Off option for Delay Until Repeat, the repeat feature will be disabled entirely.

*Mouse (or Trackpad, if you have a PowerBook or iBook)*
This panel lets you specify the mouse's Tracking Speed, as well as the delay between double-clicks. If you are using an iBook or PowerBook, the Mouse preferences panel will have an added section for setting the controls for your trackpad.

*Bluetooth*
This pane is used to configure the settings for Apple's Bluetooth keyboard and mouse, if you have them. The Mouse and Keyboard sections have indicators to show the battery level for each device.

*Keyboard Shortcuts*
This panel lists the various keyboard shortcuts that you can use on your Mac. You can also add, remove, or change the shortcuts to suit your needs.

At the bottom of this window is a checkbox item for turning on keyboard access. If you click on the Full Keyboard Access tab and opt to "Turn on full keyboard access," you can use the Control key with either Function keys, Letter keys, or Custom keys instead of using the mouse. These key combinations and their functions are listed in Table 8.

*Table 8. Keyboard Access key combinations*

| Function keys | Letter keys | Description |
| --- | --- | --- |
| Control-F1 | Control-F1 | Enable/disable keyboard access |
| Control-F2 | m | Control the menu bar |
| Control-F3 | d | Control the Dock |
| Control-F4 | w | Activate the window or the next window behind it |

*Table 8. Keyboard Access key combinations (continued)*

| Function keys | Letter keys | Description |
|---|---|---|
| Control-F5 | t | Control an application's toolbar |
| Control-F6 | u | Control an application's utility window (or palette) |
| Control-F7 | Control-F7 | Used for windows and dialogs to highlight either text input fields and lists, or for any window control |
| Esc | Esc | Return control to the mouse, disabling the Control-F*x* key combination |
| Spacebar | Spacebar | Perform the function of a mouse click |

### TIP

If you are using an iBook or PowerBook, you need to use Control plus the *fn* key along with the Function or Letter key for keyboard access; for example, Control-fn-F2 to access menus. The *fn* key is at the bottom-left corner of your keyboard, to the left of the Control key (and below the Shift key).

*Print & Fax*

This panel is used to configure printers and set up your Mac to accept faxes. From the Faxing pane, you can opt to have incoming faxes saved to a directory, emailed to you, or sent to a printer.

*Sound*

This panel offers two panes, one for configuring Alert sounds and another for sound Output (e.g., speakers). The Alerts pane has an option for including a volume control slider in the menu bar.

## Internet & Network

These panels described next are used to control your Mac's settings for connecting to other computers.

*.Mac*

This panel has two tabbed panes, .Mac and iDisk, which allow you to configure the settings for your .Mac account (formerly known as iTools) and supply you with information about your iDisk (requires a .Mac account).

*Network*

This panel is used to configure your settings for dial-up, Ethernet, AirPort, and Bluetooth networking, including enabling/disabling AppleTalk. For details on how to configure these settings, see Part V.

*QuickTime*

This panel lets you configure QuickTime's settings for playing back movies and music. If you've purchased a license for QuickTime Pro, click on the Registration button to enter the registration number.

*Sharing*

The Sharing panel is used to set the name of your computer and your Rendezvous name. The lower portion of the Sharing panel has three tabbed panes:

*Services*

This pane allows you to turn on file, web, and printer sharing, control FTP access to your machine, and allow users of other computers to log into your machine remotely via the Secure Shell (SSH).

*Firewall*

By default, the firewall is turned off. Use this panel to restrict people from the outside world from gaining access to your machine through its various ports and services. The services you turn on in the Services pane control the enabled services in the Firewalls pane. For example, if you turn on Personal File Sharing in the Services pane, the checkbox next to Personal Fire Sharing will be checked in the Firewall pane.

*Internet*

> This pane allows you to share your Internet connection with other computers, via either AirPort or built-in Ethernet.

## System

The items in the System panel allow you to configure a variety of settings for your computer:

*Accounts*

> As the name implies, this panel is used to add and remove users and to make changes to their identities and passwords.
>
> If you have administrator privileges, you can also specify Limitations of a nonadministrator's account, for doing such things as removing items from the Dock, using the System Preferences, changing passwords, burning CDs or DVDs, and even restricting which applications and utilities are available to the user.

*Classic*

> Use this to start, stop, and restart the Classic environment. For additional information, see "Mac OS X and the Classic Environment," earlier in this book.

*Date & Time*

> This panel is used to set the date, time, and time zone for your system, specify a network time server, and specify how (or whether) the date and time will appear in the menu bar.

*Software Update*

> As with Mac OS 9, the Software Update panel can be used to check for updates to your Mac OS X system. You can use this panel to check for updates manually (i.e., when you want to, or when you learn of an available update) or automatically (daily, weekly, or monthly). When an update is found, you will be prompted to specify which updates will be downloaded and installed on your system.

New to Panther is the "Download important updates in the background" feature. If you mark this checkbox, Software Update automatically downloads and installs important updates for you.

---

**TIP**

You can also launch Software Update from the Apple menu and the About This Mac panel.

---

*Speech*

This panel can be used to turn on and configure speech recognition, specify a default voice for applications that speak text, and specify whether items in the user interface (such as alert messages or the text in menus) will be spoken as well.

*Startup Disk*

This panel is used to specify whether your system will boot into Mac OS 9 or Mac OS X. With Panther, you can also specify a Network Startup disk if your computer is configured or set up via NetBoot from Mac OS X Server.

*Universal Access*

The Universal Access panel provides support for people with disabilities. Panther features two panes, for people who have problems Seeing or Hearing, and includes two additional panes for those who find it difficult to use a Keyboard or Mouse.

One thing you'll quickly notice is that all the text labels for the user interface elements in the Universal Access panel are spoken using the voice you've specified in the Speech panel.

To quit the System Preferences application, you can use either ⌘-Q or ⌘-W. (Yes, closing the System Preference window quits the application.)

---

# Applications and Utilities

Apple has included a set of native applications and utilities for Mac OS X, including the famous suite of iApps (iMovie, iPhoto, iTunes, iCal, and iSync).

There are applications for such things as viewing and printing PostScript and PDF files, basic word processing, sending and receiving email, and creating movies, as well as utilities to help you manage your system.

Use the Finder to locate the applications (*/Applications*) and utilities (*/Applications/Utilities*) on your system. You can quickly go to the Applications folder either by clicking on the Applications icon in the Sidebar or by using the Shift-⌘-A keyboard shortcut. To quickly get to the Utilities folder, you might consider dragging the Utilities folder icon to the Finder's Sidebar, or use its keyboard shortcut, Shift-⌘-U.

## Applications

The following is a list of the programs found in the Applications directory:

*Address Book*
> This is a database program you can use to store contact information for your friends and colleagues.

*AppleScript*
> This folder contains all the tools necessary for writing AppleScripts. If you've downloaded or installed the Xcode Tools (see "Xcode Tools"), you will also have the ability to build applications using AppleScript Studio.

*Calculator*
> The Calculator is a fully functional scientific calculator. Calculator also has a Paper Tape sheet that allows you to view the math functions, which you can copy and paste into another document window.

*Chess*

Based on GNU Chess, Apple has taken this Unix-based chess game and packaged it with a Cocoa interface and 3D game pieces.

*DVD Player*

If your hardware natively supports DVD playback, the DVD Player will be installed. You can use this application to view DVD movies on your Mac.

*Font Book*

New to Panther, the Font Book application offers an intuitive way to preview the fonts on your Mac, as well as the ability to create font collections.

*iCal*

iCal is a calendaring application (similar to Entourage, if you're a Windows convert), which allows you to manage and publish your calendar to any WebDAV-enabled server (including your .Mac account). You can also subscribe to other calendars (such as a listing of holidays, the schedule for your favorite sports team, or another user's calendar).

*iChat*

This is the new chat client. iChat allows you to chat with other .Mac members, as well as with AOL Instant Messenger (AIM) users. iChat also supports messaging via Rendezvous, for dynamically finding iChat users on your local network.

If you have an iSight camera, you can also use iChat for video conferencing over the Internet. To learn more about iSight, visit Apple's web site at *http://www.apple.com/ isight*.

*Image Capture*

This program can be used to download pictures and video from a digital camera to your Mac. New in Panther, you can share input devices such as digital cameras and scanners attached to your Mac with other users on a network.

To enable device sharing, go to Image Capture → Preferences (or ⌘-,) → Sharing, then click on the checkbox next to "Share my devices".

*iMovie*

Use iMovie to create digital movies on your Mac. To learn more about iMovie, see *iMovie 3 & iDVD: The Missing Manual* (Pogue Press/O'Reilly), or go to Apple's page at *http://www.apple.com/imovie*.

*Internet Connect*

This application is used for connecting to the Internet or to another computer via a dial-up modem or an AirPort connection. You can use Internet Connect to connect your Mac to a Virtual Private Network (VPN) via File → New VPN Connection. In Panther, Internet Connect supports PPTP (Point-to-Point Tunneling Protocol) and L2TP (Layer 2 Tunneling Protocol) over IPSec for connecting to a VPN.

Internet Connect shows your current dial-up status and settings (as configured in the Network pane of your System Preferences) and provides a Connect/Disconnect button for opening or closing a connection.

*Internet Explorer*

Microsoft's Internet Explorer 5.2.1 web browser.

---

**TIP**

Now that we have Safari for browsing the Web, you can opt not to install Internet Explorer when installing Panther on your Mac. That, or you can always drag it to the Trash (where it belongs).

---

*iPhoto*

iPhoto allows you to download, organize, and edit images taken with a digital camera. iPhoto is much more powerful than Image Capture (described earlier). To learn more about iPhoto, see *iPhoto 2: The Missing Manual* (Pogue Press/O'Reilly) or Apple's iPhoto page at *http://www.apple.com/iphoto*.

*iSync*

iSync can be used to synchronize data—contact information from your Address Book, your iCal calendars, music, etc.—from your computer to another device such as a cellular phone, PDA, iPod, or another computer.

*iTunes*

iTunes can be used to play CDs, listen to Internet radio stations, import (rip) music from CDs, burn CDs from music you've collected, and store and play MP3 files. If you have an iPod, you can also use iTunes to synchronize your MP3 music files.

iTunes also serves as the virtual storefront for the iTunes Music Store (ITMS). If you have an Apple account, you can use the ITMS to purchase AAC-encoded music files for $.99 each. For more information about the iTunes Music Store, visit Apple's page at *http://www.apple.com/music/store*

*Mail*

This is the default email client for Mac OS X.

*Preview*

Preview received a major revision with Panther and is now more than just a simple image viewer or PDF reader. Preview lets you open (and export) files that have been saved in a variety of image formats—including PICT, GIF, JPEG, and TIFF, to name a few—and can also be used to view raw PostScript files. Preview can also be used to open and view PDF files, the standard format now for the screenshots you create with Shift-⌘-3 or Shift-⌘-4.

*QuickTime Player*

This is used for playing QuickTime movies, as well as listening to QuickTime streaming audio and video.

*Safari*

Safari is a fast Cocoa-based web browser, built by Apple specifically for Mac OS X. Safari is the default web browser that ships with Panther; if you want to use some other browser as the default, you can change this in Safari's preferences (Safari → Preferences → General → Default Web Browser).

## Sherlock

Sherlock 3 is Apple's venture into web services. (As mentioned earlier, the search functionality has been built into the Finder, and indexing is done via the Get Info window for drives, partitions, and folders.) To use Sherlock, you *must* have a connection to the Internet. Sherlock 3 can be used to conduct searches on the Internet for:

- Pictures
- Stock quotes
- Movie theaters and show times
- Locating a business in your area (based on the address information you provide in Sherlock's preferences), along with driving directions and a map to the location
- Bidding on eBay auction items
- Checking the arrival and departure times of airline flights
- Finding the definition or spelling for a word in the dictionary
- Searching in AppleCare's Knowledge Base to solve a problem you're having with your computer
- Getting a quick translation from one language to another

## Stickies

Stickies is a simple application that lets you create sticky notes on your screen. Like the notes stuck to your desk or computer, Stickies can be used to store important notes and reminders.

## System Preferences

This is the System Preferences application, described earlier and throughout this book.

*TextEdit*

TextEdit also received a bit of an upgrade for Panther and is the default application for creating text and rich text documents. TextEdit now sports a ruler bar with text-formatting buttons for changing the alignment, leading, and indentation of text. By default, TextEdit documents are saved rich text format (*.rtf* and *.rtfd*), but you can also save documents as plain text (*.txt*) via the Format → Make Plain Text menu option. TextEdit replaces the SimpleText application from earlier versions of the Mac OS.

Best of all, TextEdit can open Word files (*.doc*), making it possible for you to read, print, and edit Word files even if you don't have Microsoft Office. However, TextEdit's compatibility with Word is limited; for example, TextEdit can't interpret Word files that use change tracking.

## Utilities

The tools found in the Utilities folder can be used to help you manage your Mac:

*Activity Monitor*

Panther's Activity Monitor combines the CPU Monitor and Process Viewer utilities from earlier versions of Mac OS X. The Activity Monitor lets you view the processes running on your system and provides a way for you to see the CPU load, how memory is allocated, disk activity, disk usage, and network activity. If you click on a process name, you can see additional information about that process, or you can cancel (*kill*, in Unix-speak) by highlighting a process and choosing Process → Quit (Option-⌘-Q).

*AirPort Admin Utility*

This utility is used to administer AirPort Base Stations.

*AirPort Setup Assistant*

This utility is used to configure your system to connect to an AirPort wireless network.

*Asia Text Extras*

> This folder contains two tools (Chinese Text Converter and IM Plugin Converter) for converting Chinese text.

*Audio MIDI Setup*

> This utility is used to add, set up, and configure Musical Instrument Digital Interface (MIDI) devices connected to your Mac.

*Bluetooth File Exchange*

> This utility allows you to exchange files with other Bluetooth-enabled devices, such as cellular phones, PDAs, and other computers. To exchange a file, launch this utility and then drag a file from the Finder to the Bluetooth File Exchange icon in the Dock. A window will appear, asking you to select a recipient (or recipients) for the file.

*Bluetooth Serial Utility*

> This utility keeps track of the serial ports used on your computer for incoming or outgoing connections with Bluetooth devices.

*Bluetooth Setup Assistant*

> This utility is used to configure Bluetooth devices (such as mice, keyboards, mobile phones, etc.) with your Mac.

*ColorSync Utility*

> This utility has four main functions. By pressing the Profile First Aid icon, it can be used to verify and repair your ColorSync settings. The Profiles icon keeps track of the ColorSync profiles for your system, and the Devices icon lets you see which ColorSync devices are connected, as well as the name and location of the current profile. The Filters icon lets you apply filters to selected items within a PDF document.

---

**TIP**

The ColorSync Utility combines features that were in the ColorSync preference panel and the Display Calibrator utility in Jaguar.

---

*Console*

One of the many system utilities to get an overhaul for Panther, the primary use of the Console application is to log the interactions between applications on your system as well as with the operating system itself. The Console gives you quick and easy access to system and crash logs via the Logs icon in its toolbar. The crash log created by the Console application can be used by developers to help debug their applications and should be supplied to Apple if you come across a bug in Mac OS X.

*DigitalColor Meter*

This small application lets you view and copy the color settings from any pixel on your screen.

*Directory Access*

This utility controls access for Mac OS X systems to Directory Services, such as NetInfo, LDAP, Active Directory, and BSD flat files, as well as Discovery Services such as AppleTalk, Rendezvous, SLP, and SMB.

*Disk Utility*

In Panther, Disk Copy and the Disk Utility have been combined. This utility now lets you create disk images (*.dmg*) for batching and sending files (including folders and applications) from one Mac user to another. It can also be used to repair a damaged hard drive, erase rewriteable media such as CD-RWs, and initialize and partition new drives.

*Grab*

This utility can be used to take screenshots of your system. Two of its most useful features include the ability to select the pointer (or no pointer at all) to be displayed in the screenshot, and the ability to start a 10-second timer before the screenshot is taken, to give you the necessary time to set up the shot.

*Installer*

This program launches whenever you install an application on your system.

*Java*

The following Java utilities can be found in this directory:

*Applet Launcher*

This utility lets you run Java applets on your Mac.

*Java Plugin Settings*

This controls Java settings when Java runs in a browser. Panther ships with two versions of this utility, one for Java 1.3.1 and another for Java 1.4.1.

*Java Web Start*

Java Web Start (JWS) can be used to download and run Java applications.

*Keychain Access*

This utility can be used to create and manage your passwords for accessing secure web and FTP sites, networked filesystems, and other items, such as password-encoded files. You can also use Keychain Access to create secure, encrypted notes that can be read only using this utility.

*NetInfo Manager*

The NetInfo Manager is mainly a tool for system and network administrators to view and edit the settings for a system. You need to have administrator privileges to use NetInfo Manager.

*Network Utility*

This utility is a graphical frontend to a standard set of Unix tools such as *netstat*, *ping*, *lookup*, *traceroute*, *whois*, and *finger*. It also lets you view specific information about your network connection, view stats about your AppleTalk connections, and scan the available ports for a particular domain or IP address.

*ODBC Administrator*

This tool allows you to connect to and exchange data with ODBC-compliant data sources. ODBC, which stands for Open Database Connectivity, is a standard database protocol, supported by most database systems such as FileMaker Pro, Oracle, MySQL, and PostgreSQL. You can use ODBC Administrator to add data sources, install new database drivers, trace calls to the ODBC API, and configure connection pooling.

*Printer Setup Utility*

This is used to configure and control the printers connected to your computer, either locally or on a network via AppleTalk, Open Directory, IP Printing, Rendezvous, USB, or Windows printing. In Panther, you can also configure printers from the Print & Fax preference panel (System Preferences → Print & Fax → Printing → Set Up Printers).

---

**NOTE**

For users who are coming over from Mac OS 9, the Printer Setup Utility replaces the Chooser for managing printers.

---

*StuffIt Expander*

This is the popular utility for expanding, or decompressing, files. To launch StuffIt Expander, simply double-click on the compressed file. StuffIt Expander can open files saved as *.bin*, *.hqx*, *.sit*, *.zip*, *.tar*, *.tar.gz*, and *.tgz*, to name a few.

*System Profiler*

This tool (formerly known as the Apple System Profiler) keeps track of the finer details about your system. Here, you can view information about your particular computer, the devices (e.g., Zip or Jaz drive, CD-ROM drives, etc.) and volumes (i.e., hard drives and partitions) connected to your Mac, as well as listings of the frameworks, extensions, and applications on your Mac.

*Terminal*

The Terminal application is the command-line interface (CLI) to Mac OS X's Unix core. For more information about the Terminal, see "Configuring and Using the Terminal," later in this book.

*X11*

This is Apple's Mac OS X–compatible distribution of the X Window System. Since X11 is something used more by long time Unix users, this utility isn't installed by default with Panther, but it is available as one of the Custom options during the install.

# Xcode Tools

Apple has gone to great lengths to lure a new breed of developers to the Mac, offering environments for traditional C, C++, Objective-C (and recently Objective-C++), Java, Perl, Python, and Ruby. With the introduction of AppleScript Studio, AppleScripters can now harness their scripting knowledge to build Cocoa-based applications.

## Installing the Xcode Tools

You can quickly check to see whether you have the Xcode Tools installed. If you have a */Developer* folder on your hard drive, you are ready to go. If not, you'll need to install the tools either from the Xcode Tools CD that came with your system or from a disk image you can download from the Apple Developer Connection (ADC) site.

The Xcode Tools CD comes with every boxed set of Mac OS X (including Mac OS X Server), as well as with new Macs shipped from the factory with Mac OS X. To install the tools, simply find the CD (it's the gray one), put it into your CD-ROM drive, and double-click the *Developer.mpkg* file that appears.

If you can't find your Xcode Tools CD, you should go to the
ADC member web site at *http://connect.apple.com* and register as an online member (it's free). Then you can download
the Xcode Tools.

To download the Tools, log in to the ADC Member web site,
click on Download Software in the navigation bar, and then
click on the Mac OS X subcategory link that appears. From
this page, you can download the Xcode Tools. The Tools will
download in segments; simply double-click on the first seg-
ment and StuffIt Expander will launch and compile all of the
segments into one file.

The Tools are provided as a Disk Image (*.dmg*) file. When
you double-click on a disk image, a temporary disk is
mounted onto your system. Simply navigate to this disk in
the Finder and double-click on the *Developer.mpkg* file to
launch the installer.

## Overview of the Xcode Tools

The Xcode Tools are installed in the */Developer/Applications*
folder, and additional tools are placed within the */Developer/
Applications/Utilities* folder. This section will briefly describe
the more commonly used tools:

*Interface Builder*

Interface Builder is a GUI editor for both Cocoa and Carbon applications. It has complete online help and release notes, available by launching Project Builder and using the Help menu.

*Xcode*

Formerly known as Project Builder, Xcode is an integrated development environment for Mac OS X. It supports both Cocoa and Carbon, using C, C++, Objective-C, and Java. Xcode also provides an interface for accessing Apple's reference documentation for the Carbon and Cocoa APIs, and it features such enhancements as code completion and distributed builds via Rendezvous.

*FileMerge*

FileMerge compares two files or directories and lets you merge them together.

*PackageMaker*

PackageMaker lets you package your software so that the Mac OS X Installer can install it on a user's machine.

*icns Browser*

The icns Browser is used to display the contents of a *.icns* file.

*IconComposer*

IconComposer is used to create icon files (*.icns*) from existing images.

*PEFViewer*

PEFViewer displays the contents of a PEF binary as a hexadecimal dump.

*Property List Editor*

The Property List Editor lets you edit and create XML property lists.

For additional information about other development tools, including command-line and Java tools, see */Developer/ Documentation/DeveloperTools/Tools.html*.

# PART IV

# Mac OS X Unix Basics

This part is a basic introduction to show new users the Unix side of Mac OS X. Specifically, this section will cover:

- Configuring and Using the Terminal
- Command-Line Editing with *bash*
- Additional Shell Commands, such as *defaults* and *open*
- Basic Unix Commands

You don't *have* to venture into the command line if you don't want to, but it's easy to be seduced by its power; this part shows you a glimpse of what's possible with just a few easy keystrokes.

## Configuring and Using the Terminal

The Terminal application (*/Applications/Utilities*) is your interface to Mac OS X's Unix shell. The Terminal can be used for everything from creating new directories (folders) and files to launching applications, and from managing and monitoring your system to programming and tweaking your system preferences.

### Terminal Settings

This section offers advice on how to configure the settings for your Terminal. Previously, you would use Terminal → Preferences to configure the Terminal's settings. However, with Panther, you'll need to use File → Show Info and change the settings from the Terminal Inspector window via the pull-down menu at the top of the window.

*Change the style of the cursor?*
    Display & Cursor Style → (Block, Underline, Vertical Bar).

*Stop the cursor from blinking?*
    Display → Cursor Style → uncheck the box next to Blink.

*Change the background color and font colors*
*of the Terminal window?*
    Color → click on the color selection boxes next to Cursor, Normal Text, Selection, and Bold Text to change the color of the cursor and text in the Terminal window. When you click on a color box, another window opens with a color wheel, which allows you to change and select a different color. To change the background color of the Terminal window, click on the color box next to "Use this background color" in the Background Settings section.

*Assign a different title to the Terminal window?*
    Window → Title.

*Assign a different title to the current Terminal window?*
    With an open Terminal window, select File → Set Title (Shift-⌘-T). The Terminal Inspector window will open with Window selected in the pull-down menu. Enter a new title for the window in the Title field, and hit Return or Tab to change the title of the current window.

*Specify the number of lines a Terminal window can contain*
*in the scrollback buffer?*
    Buffer → Buffer Size. You can either specify a number of lines in the field provided (10,000 lines is the default), or select from an unlimited scrollback or no scrollback at all.

*Set the Terminal's emulation mode to VT100?*
    Emulation → Strict VT-100 keypad behavior.

*Close the Terminal window after I've exited?*

Shell → When the shell exits → (select from either "Close the window" or "Close only if the shell exited cleanly").

*Where is the history file for the shell?*

It's located in your Home directory as *.bash_history*. The history file keeps track of recently entered commands, which you can recall in a variety of ways, the easiest of which is to use the Up or Down Arrows to go back or forward in the history file, respectively.

*Where is bash's configuration file located?*

In */private/etc/profile*.

## Keyboard Shortcuts

Table 9 lists the keyboard shortcuts that can be used with the Terminal application.

*Table 9. Keyboard shortcuts for use with the Terminal*

| Key command | Description |
| --- | --- |
| ⌘-. (period) | Terminate process (same as Control-C, the Unix interrupt command) |
| ⌘-Up Arrow | Scroll up one line at a time |
| ⌘-Down Arrow | Scroll down one line at a time |
| ⌘-Left Arrow | Go to previous Terminal window |
| ⌘-Right Arrow | Go to next Terminal window |
| ⌘-Page Up[a] | Scroll up one screen at a time |
| ⌘-Page Down[a] | Scroll down one screen at a time |
| ⌘-Home[a] | Scroll backward to the top of the screen |
| ⌘-End[a] | Scroll forward to the bottom of the screen |
| ⌘-A | Select all the text in the Terminal window, including the scrollback |
| Shift-⌘-C | Use to open or close the Colors window |
| ⌘-I | Open the Terminal Inspector, which allows you to change some of the Terminal's settings |

*Table 9. Keyboard shortcuts for use with the Terminal (continued)*

| Key command | Description |
| --- | --- |
| ⌘-K | Clear all the information from the Terminal window, disabling scrollback (this is different and more extensive than the *clear* command, described later) |
| ⌘-N | Open new Terminal window |
| Shift-⌘-N | Run a command in a new Terminal window |
| Shift-⌘-K | Make a connection to a remote server via SSH, SFTP, FTP, or Telnet |
| ⌘-S | Save the settings of the Terminal window as a *.term* file |
| Shift-⌘-S | Save the settings of the Terminal window as a differently named *.term* file |
| Option-⌘-S | Save the contents of the Terminal window, including any scrollback, as a text file |
| Shift-Option-⌘-S | Save any selected text in the Terminal window as a text file |
| ⌘-T | Open the Font panel so you can change the Terminal's default font settings, including the font family, size, and color |
| ⌘-*number* | Switch to a different Terminal window, based on its *number* |

a  Since iBooks and PowerBooks don't have a full keyboard with the Page Up, Page Down, Home, and End keys, substitute the function key (fn) for the Command key (⌘) and use the Up, Down, Left, and Right Arrow keys, respectively, to invoke these functions.

If you're security conscious (aren't we all these days?), you might want to consider enabling the Secure Keyboard Entry option, located in the Terminal's File menu. When you enable this feature, it keeps other applications (either on your Mac or over a network) from picking up the commands (and passwords) you type into the Terminal. Even if you're using SSH to make a network connection, it never hurts to have a little more security on your side to protect your passwords and your data.

# Command-Line Editing with bash

Mac OS X's default user shell, *bash*, lets you move your cursor around in the command line, editing the line as you type. There are two main modes for editing the command line, based on the two most commonly used text editors: Emacs and vi. *bash* starts interactively in Emacs mode by default, but you can switch between modes with:

set -o emacs
    Select Emacs bindings

set -o vi
    Select vi bindings

The main difference between the Emacs and vi bindings is that the Emacs bindings are modeless (i.e., they always work). With the vi bindings, you must switch between Insert and Command modes; different commands are useful in each mode. Additionally:

- Emacs mode is simpler; vi mode allows finer control.
- Emacs mode allows you to cut text and set a mark; vi mode does not.
- The command-history-searching capabilities differ.

## Emacs Mode

Tables 10 through 14 describe the various editing keystrokes available in Emacs mode.

*Table 10. Cursor-positioning commands (Emacs mode)*

| Command | Description |
| --- | --- |
| Control-A | Move the cursor to the beginning of the line |
| Control-E | Move the cursor to the end of the line |
| Control-B | Move the cursor back (left) one character |
| Control-F | Move the cursor forward (right) one character |
| Esc-B | Move the cursor back one word |
| Esc-F | Move the cursor forward one word |

*Table 11. Text-deletion commands (Emacs mode)*

| Command | Description |
| --- | --- |
| Del or Control-H | Delete the character to the left of the cursor |
| Control-D | Delete the character under the cursor |

*Table 11. Text-deletion commands (Emacs mode) (continued)*

| Command | Description |
| --- | --- |
| Esc-D | Delete the next word |
| Esc-Delete or Esc-Control-H | Delete the previous word |
| Control-K | Delete from the cursor to the end of the line |
| Control-U | Delete the entire line |

*Table 12. Moving around in the history file (Emacs mode)*

| Command | Description |
| --- | --- |
| Control-P or Up Arrow | Recall the previous command from history |
| Control-N or Down Arrow | Recall the next command from history |
| Esc-< | Move to the first line of the history file |
| Esc-> | Move to the last line of the history file |
| Control-R | Search through the history file for a previously issued command |

*Table 13. Command completion (Emacs mode)*

| Command | Description |
| --- | --- |
| Tab | Attempt to complete the partial command entered |
| Esc-? | List the possible completions |
| Esc-/ | Attempt filename completion |
| Control-X / | List the possible filename completions |
| Esc-~ | Attempt username completion |
| Control-X ~ | List the possible username completions |
| Esc-$ | Attempt variable completion |
| Control-X $ | List the possible variable completions |
| Esc-@ | Attempt hostname completion |
| Control-X @ | List the possible hostname completions |
| Esc-! | Attempt command completion |

*Table 13. Command completion (Emacs mode) (continued)*

| Command | Description |
|---------|-------------|
| Control-X ! | List the possible command completions |
| Esc-Tab | Attempt completion from previous commands found in the history file |

*Table 14. Miscellaneous commands (Emacs mode)*

| Command | Description |
|---------|-------------|
| Control-J | Same as Return |
| Control-L | Clear the screen, placing the command prompt at the top of the Terminal window (same as ⌘-K) |
| Control-M | Same as Return |
| Control-T | Transpose two characters on either side of the cursor |
| Control-U | Delete the line from the beginning to the cursor |
| Control-[ | Same as hitting Esc |
| Esc-C | Capitalize the word following the cursor |
| Esc-U | Change the word after the cursor to all capital letters |
| Esc-L | Change the word after the cursor to all lowercase letters |
| Esc-. | Insert the last word of the previous command after the cursor |
| Esc-_ | Same as Esc-. |

## vi Mode

vi mode has two submodes: Insert mode and Command mode. The default mode is Insert. You can toggle between the modes by pressing Esc; alternatively, in Command mode, typing a (append) or i (insert) will return you to Insert mode.

Tables 15 through 21 describe the editing keystrokes available in vi mode.

*Table 15. Editing commands (vi Input mode)*

| Command | Description |
|---------|-------------|
| Delete | Delete the previous character |
| Control-W | Delete the previous word |

*Table 15. Editing commands (vi Input mode) (continued)*

| Command | Description |
| --- | --- |
| Control-V | Quote the next character |
| Esc | Enter control mode |
| i | Insert text before the cursor until Esc is pressed |
| a | Insert text after the cursor until Esc is pressed |
| I (uppercase letter I [or "eye"]) | Insert text at the beginning of the line until Esc is pressed |
| A | Insert text at the end of the line until Esc is pressed |
| R | Overwrite the existing text on the command line until Esc is pressed |

*Table 16. Commands available (vi Insert and Command mode)*

| Command | Description |
| --- | --- |
| Control-P or Up Arrow | Recall the previous command from history |
| Control-N or Down Arrow | Recall the next command from history |

*Table 17. Cursor-positioning commands (vi Command mode)*

| Command | Description |
| --- | --- |
| h | Move the cursor left one character |
| l (lowercase letter l [or "ell"]) or Spacebar | Move the cursor right one character |
| w | Move the cursor right one word |
| b | Move the cursor left one word |
| e | Move the cursor to the end of the current word |
| W, B, E | Like w, b, and e, but treat whitespace as a word separator instead of any nonalphanumeric character |
| ^ | Move the cursor to the beginning of the line (first nonwhitespace character) |
| 0 | Move the cursor to the beginning of the line |
| $ | Move the cursor to the end of the line |

Table 18. Text-deletion commands (vi Command mode)

| Command | Description |
| --- | --- |
| x | Delete the character under the cursor |
| X or Delete | Delete the character to the left of the cursor |
| dm | Delete from the cursor to the end of motion command m |
| D | Delete from the cursor to the end of the line (similar to issuing d$) |
| Control-W | Delete the previous word |
| Control-U | Delete from the beginning of the line to the cursor |
| Control-K | Delete from the cursor to the end of the line |

Table 19. Text-replacement commands (vi Command mode)

| Command | Description |
| --- | --- |
| cm | Change the characters from the cursor to the end of motion command m until Esc is pressed |
| C | Change the correct word to whatever you type (similar to issuing c$) |
| rc | Replace the character under the cursor with the character c |
| R | Replace multiple characters until Esc is pressed |
| s | Substitute the character under the cursor with the characters typed until Esc is pressed |

Table 20. Character-seeking motion commands
(vi Command mode)

| Command | Description |
| --- | --- |
| fc | Move the cursor to the next instance of c in the line |
| Fc | Move the cursor to the previous instance of c in the line |
| tc | Move the cursor just after the next instance of c in the line |
| Tc | Move the cursor just after the previous instance of c in the line |
| ; | Repeat the previous f or F command |
| , | Repeat the previous f or F command in the opposite direction |

Table 21. Searching the history file (vi Control mode)

| Command | Description |
| --- | --- |
| k or – | Move backward one line |
| j or + | Move forward one line |
| G | Move to the line given by the repeat count |
| /string | Search backward for string |
| ?string | Search forward for string |
| n | Repeat the search in the same direction as previous |
| N | Repeat the search in the opposite direction as previous |
| ! | Start a history substitution |
| !! | Refer to the last command issued |
| !n | Refer to the command line n |
| !-n | Refer to the current command line minus n |
| !string | Refer to the most recent command starting with string |
| !?string? | Refer to the most recent command containing string. The ending ? is optional. |
| ^string1^string2 | Repeat the last command, replacing string1 with string2 |

## Additional bash Shortcuts

As was just illustrated, the *bash* shell offers dozens of special keystroke characters for navigation on the command line. Table 22 lists some additional command-line keys for use in either Emacs or vi editing mode.

Table 22. Additional bash shortcuts

| Key command | Description |
| --- | --- |
| Control-C | Interrupt the process; cancels the previous command (⌘-. works as well). |
| Control-D | Used to signal end of input; will terminate most programs and return you to the shell prompt. If Control-D is issued at a shell prompt, it will close the Terminal window. |
| Control-L | Clear the display (same as typing *clear* and hitting Return). |

*Table 22. Additional bash shortcuts (continued)*

| Key command | Description |
|---|---|
| Esc-Esc | If only a partial path or filename is entered, pressing the Esc key twice will complete the name. (Pressing the Esc key twice is the same as pressing the Tab key once.) |
| Tab | Has the same effect as pressing the Esc key twice. |

# Additional Shell Commands

One of the first things that traditional Unix users will notice when they start poking around in the Terminal is that there are a few new commands they'll need to add to their repertoire. Two that we'll discuss here are *defaults* and *open*.

## defaults

When you customize your Mac using the System Preferences or an application's preferences, all those changes and settings are stored in what's known as the *preferences system*, and the command-line utility to change your preferences is the *defaults* command. Everything that you've done to make your Mac your own is stored as XML data in the form of a *property list* (or *plist*). Your property lists are stored in *~/Library/ Preferences*.

---

### WARNING

Using the *defaults* command is not for the foolhardy. If you're uncomfortable with the command line or unsure of how to change a setting properly, you should stick to using the application's Preferences pane, rather than use the *defaults* command.

If you do manage to mangle your settings, the easiest way to correct the problem is to go back to that application's Preferences pane and reset your preferences. Another solution is to delete the preferences file for the application from *~/Library/Preferences*.

---

Every time you change one of those settings, that particular property list is updated. For the initiated, there are two other ways to alter the property lists. The first is by using the Property List Editor application (*/Developer/Applications*), and the other is by using the *defaults* command in the Terminal. Extensive coverage of both is beyond the scope of this book, but we'll show you a few basic examples of how to use the *defaults* command.

## Examples

The following are some examples of working with the *defaults* command:

*View all the user defaults on your system*

```
$ defaults domains
```

This prints a listing of all the *domains* in the user's defaults system. The lists you'll see are run together with spaces in between—not quite the prettiest way to view them.

*View the settings for your Dock*

```
$ defaults read com.apple.dock
```

This reads the settings from the *com.apple.dock.plist* file, found in *~/Library/Preferences*. This listing is rather long, so you might want to the output to *less* or *more* to view the contents one screen at a time:

```
$ defaults read com.apple.dock | more
```

*Change the location of your Dock to the top of the screen*

Near the beginning of that listing, look for the following:

```
orientation = bottom;
```

You'll see that its value is set to bottom, which means that your Dock is located at the bottom of the screen. To change that setting, try the following:

```
$ defaults write com.apple.dock orientation top
```

After a short pause, you'll be returned to another command prompt, but you'll notice that the Dock is still located at the bottom of the screen. Unlike some other changes you make with the *defaults* command, changes to the Dock will take effect only if you log out and log back in.

Enter *exit* and quit the Terminal, and then save any changes in other applications and quit them too. Now log out and log back in to your system (Apple → Log Out). When you log back in, you'll see the Dock in all its glory floating just below the menu bar at the top of the screen. To quickly change its location back to the bottom of the screen (or the left or right side), use Apple → Dock → Position on (Left, Bottom, or Right).

For additional options and to learn more about how to use the *defaults* command, enter *defaults -help* or view the defaults manpage (*man defaults*).

## open

With Mac OS X, you can launch any application from the command line using the *open* command. There are three ways to invoke the command:

open [*filename*]
> This opens the file and its associated application if it isn't already running. For example:
>
> > $ **open textFile.txt**
>
> opens the file *textFile.txt* using the default text editor, which is TextEdit.

open -a [*application_path*] [*filename*]
> The *-a* option lets you specify the application to use when opening the file. For example, let's say you have both Microsoft Office 2001 and Office v.X on your system and you want to open a Word file using Word 2001. If you use open *filename.doc*, Word v.X will launch. To open the file with Word 2001, you need to do the following:

```
$ open -a /Volumes/Mac\ OS\ 9/Applications\ \(Mac\ ↵
OS\ 9\)/Microsoft\ Office\ 2001/Microsoft\ Word ↵
~/Documents/filename.doc
```

While that might look ugly (and it is), the command
does work. In this case, Classic would also launch,
because Word 2001 is a Classic app.

---

**TIP**

There is a shortcut for inserting long pathnames such as
the one shown in this example: locate the application in
the Finder, and drag the application icon from the Finder
window to the Terminal window after typing *open -a* at
the command line. The path for the application will be
inserted after the command, and then you need only tack
on the path and filename for the file.

---

open -e [*filename_path*]

The *-e* option forces the use of the TextEdit application.
For example:

```
$ open -e ~/Books/Templates/proposal_template.txt
```

Some additional examples of using the Terminal to open files
and launch applications are shown here:

*Open an HTML page using a browser other than Safari?*

The way to do this is to specify the application, using the
*-a* option:

```
$ open -a /Applications/Camino.app Sites/index.html
```

The *-a* option is used to launch Camino (formerly known
as Chimera), assuming you have Camino installed on
your system (*http://www.mozilla.org/projects/camino*) for
viewing the *index.html* file, located in your Sites directory.

*Launch Classic from the Terminal?*

If you find that you're using the Classic environment,
one way you can launch Classic from the Terminal is
with the following:

```
$ open /System/Library/CoreServices/Classic\ ↵
Startup.app
```

---

Though that does the trick, a faster way to do this is to set up an *alias* in the shell. To do so, enter the following on the command line:

```
$ alias classic='open -a /System/Library/ ↵
CoreServices/Classic\ Startup.app'
```

# Basic Unix Commands

If you've never used Unix before, this section will serve as a quick introduction to issuing Unix commands from the Terminal. Experienced Unix users can skip over this section. For each of the following, you will need to be using the Terminal application. The commands you need to type are shown in bold.

*View a command's description and its options?*

All the Unix commands on your system have a manual page (or *manpage* for short). To view the manpage for any command, you use the *man* command:

```
[MacPanther:~] chuck$ man pwd
```

The instructions for using the *pwd* command (described next) are then displayed one screen at a time. If there is more than one screen for a command's description, you will see a percentage at the lower-left corner of the Terminal window telling you how much of the manpage has been viewed. To scroll to the next screen, hit the spacebar; you will be returned to the command prompt when you've reached the end of the manpage. Even the *man* command has its own manpage, which can be viewed by using:

```
[MacPanther:~] chuck$ man man
```

*Where am I?*

Type *pwd* on the command line and hit Return; this will tell you the present working directory:

```
[MacPanther:~] chuck$ pwd
/Users/chuck
[MacPanther:~] chuck$
```

*Change directories?*

Use the *cd* command and go to the Utilities directory:

```
[MacPanther:~] chuck$ cd /Applications/Utilities
[MacPanther:/Applications/Utilities] chuck$
```

*Go back a directory?*

Use the *cd* command, followed by two dots:

```
[MacPanther:/Applications/Utilities] chuck$ cd ..
[MacPanther:/Applications] chuck$
```

*Return to where you were before the last cd command?*

Use the *cd* command, followed by a hyphen:

```
[MacPanther:/Applications] chuck$ cd -
[MacPanther:/Applications/Utilities] chuck$
```

*Go back one or more directories?*

Use the *cd* command with two dots and a slash (../ ) for each directory you want to go back. For example, to go back two directories:

```
[MacPanther:/Applications/Utilities] chuck$ cd ../..
[MacPanther:/] chuck$
```

*List a directory's contents?*

This is accomplished using the *ls* command (see Figure 15).

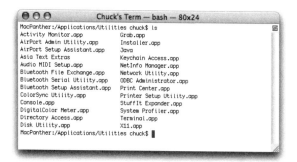

*Figure 15. Listing a directory's contents with ls*

By itself, the *ls* command creates a horizontal list of a directory's contents. Add the *-l* option to create a vertical list of a directory's contents, which also reveals more details about the file, directory, or application (see Figure 16).

```
000                Chuck's Term — bash — 80x30
MacPanther:/Applications/Utilities chuck$ ls -l
total 8
drwxrwxr-x  3 root  admin  102 15 Oct 16:36 Activity Monitor.app
drwxrwxr-x  3 root  admin  102 15 Oct 16:36 AirPort Admin Utility.app
drwxrwxr-x  3 root  admin  102 15 Oct 16:36 AirPort Setup Assistant.app
drwxrwxr-x  6 root  admin  204 15 Oct 16:36 Asia Text Extras
drwxrwxr-x  3 root  admin  102 15 Oct 16:36 Audio MIDI Setup.app
drwxrwxr-x  3 root  admin  102 15 Oct 16:36 Bluetooth File Exchange.app
drwxrwxr-x  3 root  admin  102 15 Oct 16:36 Bluetooth Serial Utility.app
drwxrwxr-x  3 root  admin  102 15 Oct 16:36 Bluetooth Setup Assistant.app
drwxrwxr-x  3 root  admin  102 15 Oct 16:36 ColorSync Utility.app
drwxrwxr-x  3 root  admin  102 15 Oct 16:36 Console.app
drwxrwxr-x  3 root  admin  102 15 Oct 16:36 DigitalColor Meter.app
drwxrwxr-x  3 root  admin  102 15 Oct 16:36 Directory Access.app
drwxrwxr-x  3 root  admin  102 27 Sep 02:52 Disk Utility.app
drwxrwxr-x  3 root  admin  102 15 Oct 16:36 Grab.app
drwxrwxr-x  3 root  admin  102 27 Sep 03:01 Installer.app
drwxrwxr-x  7 root  admin  238 15 Oct 16:36 Java
drwxrwxr-x  3 root  admin  102 15 Oct 16:36 Keychain Access.app
drwxrwxr-x  3 root  admin  102 15 Oct 16:36 NetInfo Manager.app
drwxrwxr-x  3 root  admin  102 15 Oct 16:36 Network Utility.app
drwxrwxr-x  3 root  admin  102 15 Oct 16:36 ODBC Administrator.app
lrwxr-xr-x  1 root  admin   25 15 Oct 16:09 Print Center.app -> Printer Setup Ut
ility.app
drwxrwxr-x  3 root  admin  102 15 Oct 16:36 Printer Setup Utility.app
drwxrwxr-x  3 root  admin  102 15 Oct 16:17 StuffIt Expander.app
drwxrwxr-x  3 root  admin  102 15 Oct 16:36 System Profiler.app
drwxrwxr-x  3 root  admin  102 15 Oct 16:36 Terminal.app
drwxrwxr-x  3 root  admin  102 15 Oct 16:38 X11.app
MacPanther:/Applications/Utilities chuck$ ▉
```

*Figure 16. Listing a directory's contents with ls -l*

To list all the contents for a directory, including the dot files (described earlier), add the *-a* option (either with or without the *l* option) (see Figure 17).

When you issue a command like *ls -la*, the contents of some directories will scroll up and you won't be able to see everything. One solution to this is to just issue the command and then use the Terminal window's scrollbar to go back up. Or, more efficiently, pipe (|) the command to *more*, which will display the contents of the directory one screen at a time (see Figure 18). The word *more* will be highlighted at the bottom of the screen. To

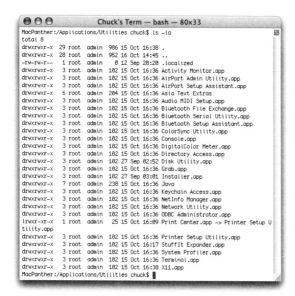

*Figure 17. Listing all a directory's contents—including dot files—using ls -la*

go to the next screen, hit the spacebar; continue doing so until you find the item you're looking for or until you reach the end.

*How can I get a listing of a directory's contents without seeing the permissions?*

Use *ls -l* and pipe the output of that listing to the *colrm* (column remove) command, as follows:

```
[MacPanther:/Applications] chuck$ ls -l | colrm 1 47
Address Book.app
AppleScript
BBEdit 7.0
Calculator.app
Chess.app
DVD Player.app
Font Book.app
Image Capture.app
```

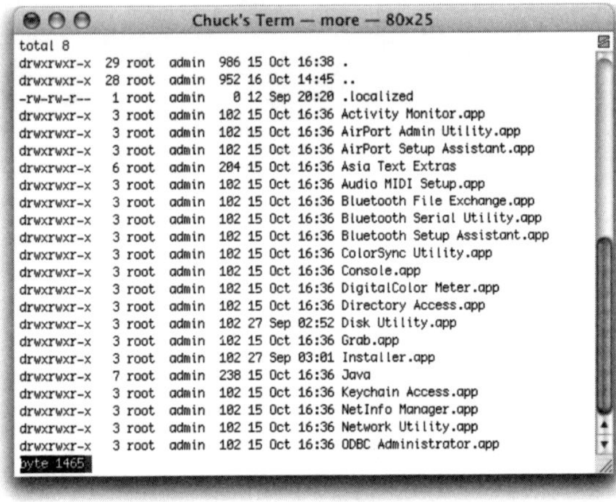

*Figure 18. Listing a directory's contents with some assistance from the more command*

```
Internet Connect.app
Mail.app
Preview.app
QuickTime Player.app
Safari.app
Sherlock.app
Stickies.app
System Preferences.app
TextEdit.app
Utilities
iCal.app
iChat.app
iMovie.app
iPhoto.app
iSync.app
iTunes.app
```

The numbers following *colrm* (1 and 47) are used by the command to specify a range of columns to remove. (A column in the Unix world is a single character. In this example, the column range of 1 through 47—all the characters preceding the file or directory name—are deleted.)

---

*Clear the display?*

When you issue the *clear* command, the Terminal window scrolls down, placing the command prompt at the top of the display:

```
[MacPanther:/Applications] chuck$ clear
```

You can also use Control-L to clear the display, and if you want to reset the Terminal window, use ⌘-K to clear the window's scrollback.

*Create a new directory (or folder)?*

Use the *mkdir* command, followed by the name of the new directory you'd like to create:

```
[MacPanther:~] chuck$ mkdir NewDirectory
```

*Remove an empty directory?*

Use the *rmdir* command:

```
[MacPanther:~] chuck$ rmdir NewDirectory
```

*Remove a directory and all its contents, including subdirectories?*

Use the *rm* command with the *-rf* option to force the removal of the directory and its contents:

```
[MacPanther:~] chuck$ rm -rf NewDirectory
```

---

#### WARNING

Notice that the *rm -rf* command will not prompt you before it deletes everything in the *NewDirectory* directory. You should use the *rm -rf* command with extreme caution, because you could delete something vital without even knowing it.

---

*Create an empty file?*

There are many ways you can do this, but one of the easiest is by using the *touch* command:

```
[MacPanther:~] chuck$ touch myfile.txt
```

*Copy a file or directory?*

Use the *cp* command:

```
[MacPanther:~] chuck$ cp myfile.txt myfile2.txt
```

This makes a copy of *myfile.txt* and creates *myfile2.txt* within the same directory. If you want to copy a file and place it in another directory, use the following:

```
[MacPanther:~] chuck$ cp myfile.txt Books/myfile.txt
```

This makes a copy of *myfile.txt* and places that copy in the */Books* directory.

## Rename a file or directory?

To rename a file, use the *mv* command:

```
[MacPanther:~] chuck$ mv myfile.txt myFile.txt
```

This renames the file *myfile.txt* to *myFile.txt* in the same directory.

## Move a file or directory?

The following moves the file *myFile.txt* to the *Books* directory:

```
[MacPanther:~] chuck$ mv myFile.txt Books
```

## See what's inside a file?

For this, you can use either *cat*, *more*, or *less*:

```
[MacPanther:~/Books] chuck$ cat myFile.txt
This is my file. I hope you like it.
Chuck
[MacPanther:~/Books] chuck$
```

## Make a file or directory read-only?

For this, you'll need to use the *chmod* (change mode) command. Any one of the following will assign read-only permission to *myFile.txt* for everyone:

```
[MacPanther:~/Books] chuck$ chmod =r myFile.txt
[MacPanther:~/Books] chuck$ chmod 444 myFile.txt
[MacPanther:~/Books] chuck$ chmod a-wx,a+r myFile.txt
```

The *chmod* command has many options; for more information, see its manpage (*man chmod*).

## Zip up a file so I can send it to a Windows user?

To zip a file or directory, use the *zip* command, as follows:

```
[MacPanther:~/Books] chuck$ zip myFile.zip myFile.txt
```

This zips up the file and places the *myFile.zip* file in the same directory as the original file.

*View the contents of a Zip file?*

Use the *unzip* command with the *-l* option to list the contents of a Zip file, as follows:

```
[MacPanther:~/Books] chuck$ unzip -l myFile.zip
Archive:  myFile.zip
 Length     Date     Time     Name
 ------     ----     ----     ----
      0   09-18-102  20:20     myFile.txt
 ------                      -------
      0                       1 file
```

This shows that there is one file in *myFile.zip* (*myFile.txt*), along with the size of the file (in kilobytes), and the date and time that the file was created.

*Unzip a file that I received from a Windows user?*

To unzip a file or directory, use the *unzip* command, as follows:

```
[MacPanther:~/Books] chuck$ unzip myFile.zip
```

This unzips the file and places its contents in the current directory. If a file with the same name is already in that directory, you will be asked what to do:

```
[MacPanther:~/Books] chuck$ unzip myFile.zip
Archive:  myFile.zip
replace myFile.txt? [y]es, [n]o, [A]ll, [N]one,
[r]ename: r
new name: myFile.txt.bak
 extracting: myFile2.txt
```

You will be given the following options to replace the existing file(s):

**y**   For yes

**n**   For no

**A**   To replace all the files with similar names

**N**   To *not* replace any of the files

**r**   To rename the like-named file that already exists

If you choose to rename the existing file (as shown in the example), you will be prompted to enter a new name for that file; enter a filename, and that file's name will be changed and the *unzip* command will extract the Zip file.

*Archive a file or directory?*

To archive a file or directory, use the Unix tape archive command, *tar*, as follows:

```
[MacPanther:~/Books] chuck$ tar cvfz myFile.tar.gz ⏎
myFile.txt
```

The options used are as follows:

*c*  Creates a new archive.

*v*  Verbose; this option prints the filenames onscreen as files that are added to or extracted from the archive.

*f*  Stores files in or extract files from an archive.

*z*  Uses *gzip* to zip, or compress, the archive.

*View the contents of a tarball?*

To peek inside a tarball to see the files it contains, use the *tar* command with the *tvfz* options:

```
[MacPanther:~/Books] chuck$ tar tvfz myFile.tar.gz
-rw-r--r--  1 chuck  staff  44 Oct 05 21:10 myFile.txt
```

The *-t* option is used to print the names of the files inside the tarball.

*Open a .tar file?*

To unpack a tarball (a *.tar* file), use the following:

```
[MacPanther:~/Books] chuck$ tar xvf myFile.tar ⏎
myFile.txt
```

The *-x* option is used to extract the contents of the tarball. This command unpacks the tarball and places its contents in the file *myFile.txt*.

If you receive a *.tgz* (or *.tar.gz*) file, that means the tarball has been compressed using *gzip*. To decompress that file, use the following command:

```
[MacPanther:~/Books] chuck$ tar xvfz myFile.tgz ⏎
myFile.txt
```

The -z option tells the *tar* command that the file it will decompress has been *gzip*'d.

*Log in as the superuser?*

Some commands require you to be the superuser (or the *root* user) before they can be issued. Rather than logging out and then logging back in as *root*, you can issue the *su* command, followed by the superuser's password:

```
[MacPanther:~] chuck$ su
Password: ********
[MacPanther:/Users/chuck] root#
```

Now you have ultimate power; use it with great care, because you could damage or overwrite something vital. When you are finished, issue the *exit* command to go back to being a normal user:

```
[MacPanther:/Users/chuck] root# exit
exit
[MacPanther:~] chuck$
```

---

**TIP**

Remember, for most (if not all) tasks, you should be able to get by with using the *sudo* command instead of logging in as *root*.

---

For more information about using the Unix side of Mac OS X, pick up a copy of *Learning Unix for Mac OS X Panther* (O'Reilly). To learn more about the *bash* shell, pick up a copy of *Learning the bash Shell* (O'Reilly).

# PART V

# Task and Setting Index

This final section of the book shows you how to configure and administer your Mac OS X system using the System Preferences and the Applications and Utilities that come with Mac OS X.

The book wraps up with a table that lists the special characters you can create from the keyboard.

## Task and Setting Index

After rooting through all the System Preferences and looking at the Applications and Utilities that come with Mac OS X, you'll quickly find that there are literally hundreds of ways to configure the settings for your system. In some cases, instructions are provided for how to perform tasks using the GUI tools and by issuing Unix commands in the Terminal. Which is faster or easier to use is up to you to decide (but you're likely to realize quickly that the power of Unix is unmatchable by most GUI tools).

This section provides shorthand instructions to help you configure and use your Mac OS X system as quickly as possible. Each task is presented as the answer to a "How do I . . . " question (e.g., How do I change the color depth of my display?), followed by the shorthand way to execute the answer (e.g., System Preferences → Displays). The tasks are divided into the following ten categories:

- Customizing the System
- Files and Folders
- Fonts and Font Management
- Searching for and Locating Files
- Obtaining Information About the System
- Internet, Web, and Email
- Modems and Dial-Up Networking
- Networking
- Printer Configuration and Printing
- Maintenance and Troubleshooting

If you're new to Mac OS X, or if you just want to jog your memory when you can't quite remember where a particular setting is located, this is the place to start.

## Customizing the System

The following are options you can use to customize the "Aqua look and feel" of your system:

*Change my desktop size/resolution, or the color depth of my display?*
   System Preferences → Displays → Display.

*Change my desktop image?*
   System Preferences → Desktop & Screen Saver → Desktop.

   Control-click on the desktop itself and select Change Desktop Background from the context menu.

*Have the pictures on my desktop change automatically?*
   System Preferences → Desktop & Screen Saver → Desktop; click on the checkbox next to "Change picture" and select an interval from the pull-down menu.

*Use one of the Mac OS 9 background images for my desktop instead of the (boring) ones that come with Mac OS X?*
   System Preferences → Desktop & Screen Saver → Desktop → Choose Folder. A Finder sheet will slide down; use

this to navigate to Mac OS 9 System Folder → Appearance → Desktop Pictures. Then, select one of the following folders and click the Choose button: *3D Graphics*, *Convergency*, *Ensemble Photos*, or *Photos*. The images in that directory will appear as part of your Desktop Collection.

*Add a new background pattern, making it available to all users?*

Create or save the image to either the *Abstract*, *Nature*, or *Solid Colors* folder in */Library/Desktop Pictures*.

*Change the double-click speed of my mouse?*

System Preferences → Keyboard & Mouse → Mouse panel.

*Change the scrolling speed for my scrollwheel mouse?*

System Preferences → Keyboard & Mouse → Mouse panel → Scrolling Speed.

*Change the settings on my iBook's trackpad so it can emulate mouse clicks?*

System Preferences → Keyboard & Mouse → Trackpad panel → Use trackpad for (Clicking, Dragging, Drag Lock).

*Change my login password?*

System Preferences → Accounts → click on your username → Password.

From the command line, use the *passwd* command.

*Change the date/time?*

System Preferences → Date & Time → Date & Time panel.

*Specify how the date and time will appear in the menu bar?*

System Preferences → Date & Time → Clock → Show the date and time.

*Specify the date and time settings for another country while I'm travelling?*

To change the date: System Preferences → International → Formats → Dates; select a country from the Region pull-down menu.

To change the time: System Preferences → International → Formats → Times; select a country from the Region pull-down menu.

*Have my Mac tell me what time it is?*

System Preferences → Date & Time → Clock → click on the checkbox next to "Announce the time" → select how frequently you'd like your Mac to announce the time from the pop-up menu.

*Use a network time server to set my clock's time?*

System Preferences → Date & Time → Date & Time; click on the checkbox next to "Set Date & Time automatically" → select an NTP Server in the scroll list.

---

**TIP**

You must be connected to the Internet to use a network time server. One helpful hint is to first use the network time server to set an accurate time for your system, then uncheck the "Set Date & Time automatically" box.

---

*Set my time zone?*

System Preferences → Date & Time → Time Zone. A map of the world will appear; simply click and drag the time-zone bar to your location on the map and let go of the mouse. As you move the time-zone bar, the date and time in the menu bar change dynamically.

*Display the current date and time from the command line?*

Use the *date* command:

```
[MacPanther:~] chuck$ date
Sun Oct 5 20:33:43 PST 2003
```

*Find out how long my system has been running?*

Use the *uptime* command:

```
[MacPanther:~] chuck$ uptime
 8:34PM  up  10:09, 2 users, load averages: 0.09, ⏎
0.12, 0.09
```

The *uptime* command displays, in the following order: the current time, how long the system has been running (*up 10:09*, or 10 hours 9 minutes), the number of users logged into the system, and the load averages on the processor.

*Change the name of my computer?*

System Preferences → Sharing; enter the new name for your computer in the Computer Name text box.

*Display the battery status for my PowerBook in the menu bar?*

System Preferences → Energy Saver; select the checkbox next to "Show battery status in menu bar."

*Display a volume control in the menu bar?*

System Preferences → Sound; select the checkbox next to "Show volume in menu bar."

*Quickly open the Sound preferences panel?*

Option-click on any one of the volume keys (mute, or volume up/down) on your keyboard.

*Automatically check for updates to the system?*

System Preferences → Software Update → Update Software; select the checkbox next to "Automatically check for updates when you have a network connection," and then select the frequency (Daily, Weekly, Monthly) from the pull-down menu.

*Have an application start up automatically after I log in?*

System Preferences → Accounts → click on your username → Startup Items. Click the Add button, and then use the Finder to select the applications you would like to have started after you log in.

Drag an application icon from the Finder to the window in the Startup Items pane in the Accounts panel.

*Adjust the amount of time my system needs to be idle before the screen saver kicks in?*

System Preferences → Desktop & Screen Saver → Screen Saver → adjust the slider next to "Start screen saver."

*Quickly activate my screen saver when I know I'll be away from my desk for a while?*

System Preferences → Desktop & Screen Saver → Screen Saver → click on the Hot Corners button at the bottom of the window. Mark a corner of the screen with a check mark to activate the screen saver when the mouse is moved to that corner. Likewise, you can enable a Hot Corner to disable the screen saver when the mouse is moved there.

*Protect my system from prying eyes while I'm away from my computer?*

System Preferences → Security → enable the checkbox next to "Require password to wake this computer from sleep or screen saver."

*Change the background of a window to a different color or to an image?*

Finder → View → as Icons, then use View → Show View Options (⌘-J); select either Color or Picture for the Background option.

*Set up my computer so it starts up or shuts down at the same time every day?*

System Preferences → Energy Saver → Schedule.

*Restart my computer automatically after a power failure?*

System Preferences → Energy Saver → Options → enable the checkbox next to "Restart automatically after a power failure."

*Enable full keyboard access so I can navigate through and select menu items without using a mouse?*

System Preferences → Keyboard & Mouse → Keyboard Shortcuts → enable the checkbox next to "Turn on full keyboard access."

## Files and Folders

The following are options for use with files and folders:

*Create a new folder?*
Control-click → New Folder (in the Finder or on the desktop).

Shift-⌘-N.

---

**TIP**

In earlier versions of the Mac OS, ⌘-N was used to create new folders; now, ⌘-N is used for opening a new Finder window.

---

*Rename a file or folder?*
Click once on the icon, and then click once on the name of the file to highlight it (or press Return). Type in the new name for the file or folder, and hit Return to accept the new name.

Click on the icon, and then use ⌘-I to open the Get Info window. Click on the disclosure triangle next to Name & Extension, and enter the new file or directory name.

In the Terminal, use the following command:

```
[MacPanther:~] chuck$ mv myFile.txt yourFile.txt
```

The *mv* command changes the name of *myFile.txt* to *yourFile.txt*.

*Change the program associated with a particular extension?*
Click on a file, and then use ⌘-I or File → Get Info. Click on the disclosure triangle next to "Open with" and select one of the applications from the pull-down menu, or choose Other to select a different program. If you want to specify that application as the default for opening files with that particular extension, click Change All; otherwise, close the Info window to save the changes.

---

*Change the permissions for a file or directory?*

Click on a file or directory, and then use ⌘-I or File → Get Info. Click on the disclosure triangle next to "Ownership & Permissions" to change the access for the Owner, Group, and Others.

Use the *chmod* command. To learn more about *chmod* and its options, see its manpage (*man chmod*).

*Copy a file to the desktop instead of moving it or creating a shortcut?*

Select the file, then Option-drag the icon to the desktop (notice a plus sign appears next to the pointer in a green bubble), and release the mouse button.

In the Finder, select the file → Edit → Copy *filename* → click on the Home icon in the Finder's sidebar → double-click on the Desktop icon → Edit → Paste item.

*Find out where an open document is saved on my system?*

Command-click on the name of the document in the titlebar. A menu will drop down from the name of the file, showing you where the file is located. If you pull down to one of the folders in that menu and release the mouse, a Finder window will open for that location.

*Create a disk image?*

To create a disk image, follow these steps:

1. Launch Disk Utility (*/Application/Utilities*).
2. In the menu bar, select Images → New → Blank Image, or click on the New Image button in Disk Utility's toolbar.
3. In the Save As field, enter a name for the disk image.
4. From the Where pop-up menu, select the location where you'd like to save the disk image.
5. Set the Size, Encryption method, and Format from their respective pop-up menus.

6. Click the Save button to create the disk image; the dial image file (with a *.dmg* file extension) will be saved in the location you selected, and the image itself will be mounted on your desktop.

7. Double-click on the disk image to open its Finder window.

8. Drag and drop the items you would like included in the disk image into the image's Finder window.

9. When complete, close the Finder window and Eject the image (⌘-E) to complete the process.

To create a disk image from an actual disk, such as your hard drive or a CD, follow these steps:

1. Launch Disk Utility (*/Application/Utilities*).

2. In the left side of Disk Utility's window, select the disk you'd like to create an image of.

3. In the menu bar, select Images → New → Image from *disk name*.

4. In the Save As field, enter a name for the image you want to create.

5. From the Where pop-up menu, select the location where you'd like to save the disk image.

6. Select the Image Format and Encryption Type from their respective pop-up menus.

7. Click the Save button to create the disk image.

*Display the contents of a shared folder on another volume in my network?*

Finder → *volume* → *folder*.

From your home directory in the Terminal:

```
[MacPanther:~] chuck$ ls -la /Volumes/volume/folder
```

*Quickly create a directory and a set of numbered directories (such as for chapters in a book)?*

```
[MacPanther:~] chuck$ mkdir -p NewBook/ ↵
{ch}{01,02,03,04,05}
[MacPanther:~] chuck$ ls -F NewBook
ch01/ ch02/ ch03/ ch04/ ch05/
```

Try doing that in the Finder—you can't! The command *ls -F NewBook* is used to list the folders within the *NewBook* directory, which shows us that five separate subdirectories have been created.

*Move a file to the Trash from the Terminal?*
```
MacPanther:~/Desktop chuck$ mv myFile.txt ~/.Trash
```

*Quickly delete a directory (and its subdirectories) without sending it to the Trash?*
```
[MacPanther:~] chuck$ rm -rf work
```

*Make the Trash stop asking me if I'm sure I want to delete every file?*
Finder → Preferences → Advanced; uncheck the option next to "Show warning before emptying the Trash."

*Empty the Trash of locked items?*
Shift-Option-⌘-Delete. The addition of the Option key forces the deletion of the contents of Trash.

*Give a file or folder a custom icon?*
Open an image file, and copy it with ⌘-C. Select the icon → File → Get Info (or ⌘-I). Select the file icon in the General section, and then paste (⌘-V) in the new image.

---

**TIP**

The proper image size for an icon is $128 \times 128$ pixels.

---

## Fonts and Font Management

Use the following options for fonts and font management:

*How can I share fonts with other users on my system?*
If you're the administrator, move the font you'd like to share from your */Users/username/Library/Fonts* folder to */Library/Fonts*.

*Where can I store new fonts I've purchased or downloaded from the Internet?*

Save them to */Users/username/Library/Fonts* for your personal use, or save them to */Library/Fonts* to allow everyone on the system access to them.

*Why aren't my bitmap fonts working?*

Mac OS X doesn't support bitmapped fonts; only True-Type, OpenType, and PostScript Level 1 fonts are supported by Mac OS X.

*What does the .dfont extension mean on some of my Mac OS X fonts?*

The extension stands for "Data Fork TrueType Font." Basically, this just tells you that this is a TrueType font.

*How can I turn off font antialiasing?*

You can't, but you can adjust the minimum font size to be affected by font smoothing in System Preferences → General → "Turn off text smoothing for font sizes *x* and smaller" (8 points is the default setting).

*How do I create a Font Collection?*

Launch the Font Book application (*/Applications*) and follow these steps:

1. Select File → New Collection (⌘-N) from the menu bar.

2. A new collection named New-0 (or some other number) appears in the Collection column; type in a different name (such as BookFonts) and hit Return.

3. In the Collection column, click on the disclosure triangle next to All Fonts, and then click on Computer; you will see a list of the installed fonts in the Font column.

4. Drag the fonts you want from the Font column and drop them onto the name of the collection you've created.

*Where are my Font Collections stored, in case I want to share them with another user?*

> */Users/username/Library/FontCollections*. If you want to share a collection, place a copy of the collection in the Shared folder. All Font Collections have a *.fcache* file extension.

## Searching for and Locating Files

The following will help you search for and locate files:

*Find a file when I don't know its name?*

> Finder → enter a keyword in the Search field in the toolbar → hit Return to start the search.
>
> Finder → File → Find (⌘-F).

*Index my hard drive to allow for content-based searching?*

> Finder → select hard drive → File → Get Info → click on the disclosure triangle next to "Content index" → click on the Index Now button.

---

### TIP

The Finder does not index filenames—only the contents of files. However, you can still search for filenames.

---

*Find a file when I can't remember where I saved it?*

> Use the *locate* command in the Terminal. However, you must first update the *locate* database as follows:
>
> ```
> [MacPanther:~] chuck$ cd /usr/libexec
> [MacPanther:/usr/libexec] chuck$ sudo ./locate. ⏎
> updatedb
> ```
>
> If you haven't built the *locate* database yet, this command could take a few minutes to run; after which, you will be returned to the command line.

Now you can use the *locate* command:

```
[MacPanther:/usr/libexec] chuck$ locate temp98.doc
/Users/chuck/Books/Templates/temp98.doc
[MacPanther:/usr/libexec] chuck$
```

In this example, I used *locate* to search for the file *temp98.doc*; in return, the command tells me in which directory it's located.

## Obtaining Information About the System

Use the following if you need to obtain system information:

*Find out how much disk space I have left?*

Launch the Finder and look in the thin bar, just below the toolbar. You will see something that says how many items are in that directory and how much space is available on your hard drive.

Issue the *df -m* command in the Terminal, as shown in Figure 19.

This shows the amount of space Used and Avail(able) for each mounted drive or partition. The / filesystem is that of Mac OS X, which on this system is at 90% capacity. Note that the numbers shown in the Used and Avail columns are listed in megabytes.

```
000                    Chuck's Term — bash — 80x24
MacPanther:~ chuck$ df -m
Filesystem          1M-blocks  Used  Avail  Capacity  Mounted on
/dev/disk0s10            5302   4739    509     90%    /
devfs                       0      0      0    100%    /dev
fdesc                       0      0      0    100%    /dev
<volfs>                     0      0      0    100%    /.vol
/dev/disk0s9            21211  19950   1260     94%    /Volumes/Jaguar
/dev/disk0s11            2098    318   1779     15%    /Volumes/Classic
automount -nsl [280]        0      0      0    100%    /Network
automount -fstab [285]      0      0      0    100%    /automount/Servers
automount -static [285]     0      0      0    100%    /automount/static
MacPanther:~ chuck$ ▮
```

*Figure 19. Using df -m to display the available disk space*

*Find out how much memory I have?*
   $\bullet$ → About This Mac.

*Find out what version of Mac OS X I'm running?*
   $\bullet$ → About This Mac.

   $\bullet$ → About This Mac; click on the version number (e.g., 10.3) to reveal the build number (e.g., 7B85).

   System Profiler (*/Applications/Utilities*) → Contents → Software → look in the System Software Overview section to see the exact build of Mac OS X.

*Find out what processor my Mac has?*
   $\bullet$ → About This Mac.

   System Profiler (*/Applications/Utilities*) → Contents → Hardware → Hardware Overview.

*What type of cache do I have and how big is it?*
   System Profiler (*/Applications/Utilities*) → Contents → Hardware → Hardware Overview.

*Find out whether a drive is formatted with HFS?*
   Disk Utility (*/Applications/Utilities*) → select the drive or partition in the left column → click on the Info button.

*Find out what programs (or processes) are running?*
   Activity Monitor (*/Applications/Utilities*).

   From the command line, use the *ps -aux* command.

   From the command line, use the *top* command.

*Display the status of the computer's used and free memory?*

Issuing the *top* command in the Terminal displays something similar to what's shown in Figure 20.

```
● ● ●                    Chuck's Term — top — 80x24
Processes:  46 total, 2 running, 44 sleeping... 114 threads           10:27:55
Load Avg:  0.08, 0.04, 0.03    CPU usage: 1.8% user, 11.7% sys, 86.5% idle
SharedLibs: num = 106, resident = 24.8M code, 2.61M data, 6.05M LinkEdit
MemRegions: num = 4452, resident = 39.5M + 9.60M private, 73.1M shared
PhysMem: 53.8M wired, 109M active, 99.7M inactive, 262M used, 505M free
VM: 3.11G + 72.0M  19573(0) pageins, 0(0) pageouts

  PID COMMAND      %CPU  TIME    #TH #PRTS #MREGS  RPRVT  RSHRD  RSIZE  VSIZE
  478 screencapt   0.0% 0:00.04   1   25    29     196K   780K   872K   91.3M
  476 top          9.9% 0:01.55   1   17    26     292K   408K   1.73M  27.1M
  474 DiskManage   0.0% 0:00.35   2  306    41     756K   1.20M  1.85M  35.7M
  473 Disk Utili   0.0% 0:03.05   4  129   183     2.64M  12.3M  9.89M  148M
  472 DiskManage   0.0% 0:00.41   2  302    41     756K   1.20M  1.85M  35.7M
  470 System Pro   0.0% 0:07.61   4  132   409     3.81M  16.0M  21.9M  168M
  462 Preview      0.0% 0:07.02   2   94   151     2.79M  8.80M  8.12M  152M
  458 bash         0.0% 0:00.03   1   12    15     152K   856K   748K   18.2M
  457 login        0.0% 0:00.02   1   13    37     140K   400K   492K   26.9M
  446 lookupd      0.0% 0:00.13   2   34    47     284K   924K   1.04M  28.5M
  442 Terminal     0.0% 0:02.38   3   64   119     1.23M  9.45M  5.30M  143M
  341 ntpd         0.0% 0:00.38   1   10    18     136K   516K   688K   17.9M
  332 BBEdit       0.0% 1:19.38   3   98   162     5.88M  16.4M  13.3M  159M
  324 Finder       0.0% 0:04.47   1   98   156     3.85M  18.8M  12.5M  161M
  323 SystemUISe   0.0% 0:01.81   2  202   238     1.35M  10.3M  5.61M  144M
  320 Dock         0.0% 0:01.21   2   78   112     660K   16.4M  7.40M  138M
```

*Figure 20. Display for the top command*

The *top* command gives you a real-time view of the processes running on your system, as well as processor and memory usage. To see how much memory you have available, look at the end of the PhysMem line; in this case, I can see that my system is using 262 megabytes (262M) of RAM and that I have 505 megabytes (505M) free. To stop the *top* command from running, hit Control-C or ⌘-. to cancel the process.

*View the hardware connected to my system?*

System Profiler (*/Applications/Utilities*). This information can be gathered from Hardware Overview section.

*Generate a report about my system so I can submit it to Apple along with a bug report?*

System Profiler (*/Applications/Utilities*) → File → Export → Plain Text; a sheet will slide out where you can assign the file a name and a place to save the file.

Now you can open, view, and print the file using Text-Edit, or copy and paste this into a bug report.

# Internet, Web, and Email

Use the following settings as they relate to your Internet, web, and email usage:

*Specify where Safari will save files downloaded from the Internet?*
   Safari → Preferences (⌘-,) → General → Save downloaded files to: → select a location in the pop-up menu.

*Change Safari's default home page?*
   Safari → Preferences (⌘-,) → General → Home page → enter a different URL in this field.

*Set up a .Mac account?*
   System Preferences → .Mac → .Mac → Sign Up. (You must be connected to the Internet to set up a .Mac account.)

*Turn on web sharing?*
   System Preferences → Sharing → Services pane. Click on the checkbox next to Personal Web Sharing to start this service. Enabling this service allows others to access your Sites folder (*/Users/username/Sites*) from the Internet. To learn more about Personal Web Sharing, point your default browser to */Users/username/Sites/index.html*. The address for your personal web site will be *http://yourIPAddress/~yourshortusername/*.

*Register my license number for QuickTime Pro?*
   System Preferences → QuickTime; click on the Registration button and enter your license number.

*Listen to an Internet radio station?*
   Dock → iTunes → Radio. Clicking on the Radio option in the Source pane to the left, the right pane will change to show you a list of different music genres from which to choose. Click on the disclosure triangle next to a music type to reveal the available stations.

*Use my own stylesheet for viewing web pages in Safari?*

Safari → Preferences (⌘-,) → Advanced → Style Sheet → Other → locate and select the Cascading Style Sheet (CSS) you want to apply.

*Download a file via FTP?*

If you've noticed, Mac OS X doesn't come with a graphical FTP client, such as the venerable Fetch program (*http://www.fetchsoftworks.com*). But why bother paying for something when you can FTP files from the command line for free? For example, if you wanted to download O'Reilly's latest Word template for authors (stored in */pub/frame/templates/mswd*), you could use FTP from the Terminal as follows:

```
[MacPanther:~] chuck$ ftp ftp.oreilly.com
Connected to ftp.ora.com.
<snip>
Name (ftp.oreilly.com:chuck): anonymous
331 Anonymous login ok, send your complete email
address as password.
Password: username@domain.com
230 Anonymous access granted, restrictions apply.
Remote system type is UNIX.
Using binary mode to transfer files.
ftp> cd pub/frame/templates/mswd
250 CWD command successful.
ftp> ls
200 PORT command successful.
150 Opening ASCII mode data connection for /bin/ls.
total 1488
-rwxr--r--   1 prod     ora         631296 ↵
Oct 14 20:15 ORA.dot
-rwxrw-r--   1 prod     ora         768512 ↵
Oct  9 19:49 ORA_Template_Instructions.doc
-rwxrw-r--   1 prod     ora         567296 ↵
Sep 29 20:48 ORA_v2_8b.dot
-rwxrw-r--   1 prod     ora         529408 ↵
Sep 30 16:20 ORA_v2_9b.dot
drwxrwxr-x   4 prod     ora           1024 ↵
Apr 15 2003 old
-rwxrw-r--   1 prod     ora         229376 ↵
May  8 21:55 temp98.doc
226 Transfer complete.
```

```
ftp> bin
200 Type set to I.
ftp> get ORA.dot
local: ORA.dot remote: ORA.dot
200 PORT command successful.
150 Opening BINARY mode data connection for ORA.dot
(631296 bytes).
226 Transfer complete.
206848 bytes received in 00:05 (119.91 KB/s)
ftp> bye
221 Goodbye.
[MacPanther:~] chuck$
```

The Word template (*ORA.dot*) will be saved in your
home directory, as noted by the path ([MacPanther:~]).
To learn more about using FTP from the command line,
see *Learning Unix for Mac OS X Panther* (O'Reilly).

Another option is to use *curl* as follows:

```
[MacPanther:~] chuck$ curl -O ftp://ftp.oreilly.com/ ⏎
pub/frame/templates/mswd/ORA.dot
```

As you can see, the *curl* command requires the entire
path to the file you want to download; the -O option tells
*curl* to save the file to a local disk. To learn more about
*curl*, see its manpage.

*Create shortcuts on my desktop for web sites I visit often, or
for people I email frequently?*
Open the TextEdit application, enter a URL (such as
*http://www.oreilly.com*) or an email address (such as
*chuckdude@mac.com*), and then triple-click on the
address to select the entire line and drag that to your
desktop. This creates an icon on your desktop for whatever you drag there. When you double-click on the icon,
your default web browser opens that URL, or your email
client creates a new message window with the address
specified by the shortcut.

*Find out how much space I have available on my iDisk?*
System Preferences → .Mac → iDisk.

*Require a password from others before they can access my
iDisk's Public folder?*

System Preferences → .Mac → iDisk. Click on the checkbox next to "Use a Password to Protect your Public
Folder," and then click on the Password button to set a
password.

*Create a local copy of my iDisk on my hard drive so I can back
it up?*

System Preferences → .Mac → iDisk → enable the checkbox next to "Create a local copy of your iDisk" → select
either Automatically or Manually for how you want to
synchronize your iDisk with your local copy.

## Modems and Dial-Up Networking

Use the following options to configure your modem and dial-
up networking:

*Configure a modem for dialing into my ISP?*

Go to System Preferences → Network, and follow these
steps:

1. Select New Location from the Location pull-down
   menu. Enter a name for the new location (for example, My ISP), and click OK.
2. Select Internal Modem from the Show pull-down
   menu.
3. Fill in the blanks on the PPP panel.
4. In the TCP/IP panel, select Using PPP from the Configure IPv4 pull-down menu.
5. Select your modem type from the Modem panel.
6. Click the Apply Now button.

*Show the modem status in the menu bar*

System Preferences → Network → select Internal Modem
from the Show pull-down menu → Modem pane; click on
the checkbox next to "Show modem status in menu bar."

*Make sure my modem is working?*
> Applications → Utilities → Internet Connect.

*Set my computer to wake up from sleep mode when the modem rings?*
> System Preferences → Energy Saver → Options → Wake Options; click on the checkbox next to "Wake when the modem detects a ring."

*Find out the speed of my dial-up connection?*
> Applications → Utilities → Internet Connect. The bottom section of the window tells you the speed of your connection.

*Disable call-waiting on my phone when using the modem?*
> System Preferences → Network → PPP. Insert *70 to the beginning of the telephone number you're dialing (e.g., *70, 1-707-555-1212).

*Where are my modem configuration files stored?*
> /Library/Modem Scripts.

*Specify how many times my modem will redial if it detects a busy signal?*
> System Preferences → Network → Show → Internal Modem → PPP panel → PPP Options → Session Options → Redial if busy → Redial x times.

## Networking

The following settings aid with networking options:

*Find the media access control (MAC) address for my Ethernet card?*
> Finder → Applications → Utilities → System Profiler → Network Contents → Configuration Name → Built-in Ethernet → look at the bottom half of the display for the "Ethernet Address."

> System Preferences → Network → Ethernet pane, look for a sequence of numbers and letters next to Ethernet Address.

*Configure my system to connect to an Ethernet network?*

Go to System Preferences → Network and follow these steps:

1. Select New Location from the Location pull-down menu. Enter a name for the new location (for example, ORA-Local), and click OK.

2. Select Built-in Ethernet from the Show pull-down menu.

3. From the Configure pull-down menu in the TCP/IP panel, select Using DHCP if your IP address will be assigned dynamically, or Manually if your machine will have a fixed IP address. (In most cases, particularly if you have a broadband Internet connection at home, your IP address will be assigned via DHCP.)

4. If you're on an AppleTalk network, select the Make AppleTalk Active option in the AppleTalk panel, and select your Zone (if any).

5. Click the Apply Now button.

*Configure my system to connect to a virtual private network (VPN)?*

Here's how to set up your Mac OS X system for connecting to a VPN:

1. Launch Internet Connect (*/Applications*). (If you haven't used Internet Connect before, you will be prompted to configure the modem settings, or a VPN connection if a modem can't be found.)

2. Click on the VPN (PPTP) icon in the toolbar.

3. In the VPN Connection window, enter the Server Address, Account name, and Password that you will use to connect to the VPN. If your VPN is on a Windows-based server, you will have to enter the domain as well; for example, *domain\chuck*.

4. Click the Connect button to try connecting to the VPN.

5. Open the Network preferences panel (System Preferences → Network) and select Location → New Location; supply a name for your VPN (such as Work VPN) and hit OK.

6. Select Show → VPN (PPTP) in the Network preferences panel.

7. In the TCP/IP tab, select Configure IPv4 → select Using PPP from the drop-down menu.

8. Click the Apply Now button on the Network preferences panel.

9. Go back to Internet Connect by clicking on its Dock icon, and select File → New VPN Connection Window (Shift-⌘-P).

10. Click on the Connect button to connect to your VPN server. (The Status indicator in this window will tell you whether you're connected.)

When you want to connect to the VPN in the future, follow these steps:

1. Apple → Location → *VPN Name* (e.g., Work VPN).

2. Launch Internet Connect (*/Applications*); if you will be using the VPN frequently, you should consider adding Internet Connect to your Dock.

3. File → New VPN Connection Window (Shift-⌘-P).

4. Click on the Connect button.

When you've completed the work you need to do over the VPN, click the Disconnect button in the VPN Connection window, quit Internet Connect, and then change your network location to your regular network setting.

*Change my Rendezvous name from my full name to something else?*

System Preferences → Sharing; enter the new name in the Rendezvous Name text box. Your Rendezvous name will have a *.local* extension; for example, *MacPanther.local*.

*Configure my AirPort settings for wireless networking?*

Follow the steps for connecting to an Ethernet network first, then use the AirPort Setup Assistant (*/Applications/Utilities*). The settings you've applied for your regular network will be applied to your AirPort settings.

*Find out the speed of my network connection?*

Network Utility (*/Applications/Utilities*) → Info panel; look next to Link Speed in the Interface Information section.

*Find out what's taking a site so long to respond?*

Applications → Utilities → Network Utility → Ping panel; enter the network address for the location (e.g., *www.macdevcenter.com* or *10.0.2.1*).

Use the *ping* command:

```
[MacPanther:~] chuck$ ping hostname
```

*Trace the route taken to connect to a web page?*

Network Utility (*/Applications/Utilities*) → Traceroute panel; enter the URL for the location.

Use the *traceroute* command:

```
[MacPanther:~] chuck$ traceroute hostname
```

*Restrict access to my computer so others can get files I make available to them?*

System Preferences → Sharing → File & Web panel. Click on the Start button in the File Sharing section to give others access to your Public folder (*/Users/username/Public*). The Public folder is read-only, which means that other people can only view or copy files from that directory; they cannot write files to it.

*Where can my coworkers place files on my computer without getting access to the rest of my system?*

With file sharing turned on, people can place files, folders, or even applications in your Drop Box, located within the Public folder (*/Users/username/Public/Drop Box*).

*Quickly switch to an AirPort network after disconnecting the Ethernet cable from my iBook?*

System Preferences → Network → Show → Active Network Ports. Click on the checkboxes next to the network ports you want to enable, and drag the ports in the list to place them in the order in which you're most likely to connect to them. (The Automatic location should do this for you, but it doesn't always work.)

*Share my modem or Ethernet connection with other AirPort-equipped Macs?*

System Preferences → Sharing → Internet panel; click on the Start button to turn Internet sharing on.

*View what's inside someone else's iDisk Public folder?*

Go → Connect to Server. At the bottom of the dialog box, type *http://idisk.mac.com/membername/Public*. Click Connect or press Return; the Public iDisk image will mount on your desktop.

---

**TIP**

Not all iDisk Public folders are created equal. An iDisk owner can choose to make her Public folder read-only, or read-write, which allows others to place files in her Public folder. The Public folder can also be password protected, which means you need to enter a password before you can mount the Public folder.

---

*Connect to a networked drive?*

Go → Connect to Server (⌘-K).

If the server to which you want to connect is part of your local area network (LAN), click on the Local icon in the left pane and select the server name to the right. If the server you want to connect to is part of your local AppleTalk network, click on the AppleTalk Network icon in the left pane and select the server or computer name to the right.

*Connect to an SMB share?*

If you need to connect to a Windows server, you will need to specify the address in the text box as follows:

```
smb://hostname/sharename
```

After clicking the Connect button, you will be asked to supply the domain to which you wish to connect and your username and password.

---

### NOTE

If you make a mistake, don't expect the error message to give you any assistance in figuring out why you weren't able to connect to the share.

---

You can speed up this process by supplying the domain and your username, as follows:

```
smb://domain;username@hostname/sharename
```

where *domain* is the NT domain name, *username* is the name you use to connect to that domain, and *hostname* and *sharename* are the server name and shared directory that you have or want access to. Now, when you click on the Connect button, all you need to enter is your password (if one is required), and the networked drive will appear on your desktop.

---

### TIP

Before pressing the Connect button, press the button with a plus sign (+) in it to add the server to your list of Favorites. This will save you time in the future if you frequently need to connect to the same drive, because you won't have to enter that address again.

---

## Printer Configuration and Printing

Use the following options for printer configuration and printing:

*Configure a printer?*

Launch Print Center (*/Applications/Utilities*), and either click on the Add button in the Printer List window or select Printer → Add Printer from the menu bar. Select how the printer is connected using the pull-down menu (AppleTalk, IP Printing, Open Directory, Rendezvous, USB, or Windows):

- If you selected AppleTalk, select the zone (if any) using the second pull-down menu, choose the printer in the lower pane, and then click the Add button.
- If you selected IP Printing, you will need to know and fill in the IP address of the printer; select the printer model, and click the Add button.
- If you selected Open Directory, you can choose a printer listed in the NetInfo Network. Select the printer name, and then click the Add button.
- If you selected Rendezvous, USB, or Windows, choose the name of the printer and the printer model, and then click the Add button.

*View the jobs in the print queue?*

Launch the Print Center → double-click on the name of the printer to see the print queue.

*Cancel a print job?*

Launch the Print Center → double-click on the printer name → click on the name of the print job → click on the Delete button.

*Halt a print job?*

Launch the Print Center → double-click on the printer name → click on the name of the print job → click on the Hold button. (Click on the Resume button to start the job where it left off.)

*Share the printer that's connected to my Mac with another user?*

System Preferences → Sharing → Services; click on the checkbox next to Printer Sharing.

*Configure my system so I can print from the command line using the Terminal?*

To do this, you must first issue the cryptic *at_cho_prn* command either with the *sudo* command or as *root*:

```
[dhcp-123-45:~] chuck$ sudo at_cho_prn
Password: ********
1  East_Ora_EtherTalk     2  West_Ora_EtherTalk
ZONE number (0 for current zone)? 1
Zone:East_Ora_EtherTalk
  1: 0002.83.9dtpenguin1:LaserWriter
  2: 0002.86.9d DODO1:LaserWriter
  3: 0002.82.9d Chicken1:LaserWriter
  4: 0002.08.9d Rheas1:LaserWriter
  5: 0002.85.9d weka1:LaserWriter
ITEM number (0 to make no selection)? 5
Default printer is:weka1:LaserWriter@East_Ora_
EtherTalk
status: idle
[dhcp-123-45:~] chuck$
```

In the example shown here, I've specified *East_Ora_EtherTalk* as my AppleTalk zone and *weka1* as my default printer for printing from the command line.

*View a list of available AppleTalk printers on my network?*

From the command line, use the *atlookup* command:

```
[dhcp-123-45:~] chuck$ atlookup
Found 156 entries in zone East_Ora_EtherTalk
0002.82.08      Chicken1:SNMP Agent
0002.82.9e      Chicken1:HP LaserJet
0002.82.9c      Chicken1:HP Zoner Responder
0002.82.9d      Chicken1:LaserWriter
0002.86.9d      DODO1:LaserWriter
0002.86.08      DODO1:SNMP Agent
0002.86.9e      DODO1:HP LaserJet
0002.86.9a      DODO1:HP Zoner Responder
0002.06.08      Kiwi:SNMP Agent
0002.06.9e      Kiwi:HP LaserJet
0002.06.9c      Kiwi:HP Zoner Responder
0002.06.9d      Kiwi:LaserWriter
0003.84.80      MacPanther:Darwin
0002.85.08      weka1:SNMP Agent
```

```
0002.85.9d        weka1:LaserWriter
0002.85.9e        weka1:HP LaserJet
0002.85.9c        weka1:HP Zoner Responder
<snip>
```

---

### WARNING

If you're on a large AppleTalk network, *atlookup* will
show you *everything*: printers, servers, computers…
*everything*. You will have to look through the output to
find the item you're looking for.

---

*Send a text file to a PostScript printer?*

For this, use the *enscript* and *atprint* commands:

```
[dhcp-123-45:~/Desktop] chuck$ enscript -p- ↵
textFile.txt | atprint
Looking for weka1:LaserWriter@East_Ora_EtherTalk.
Trying to connect to weka1:LaserWriter@East_Ora_
EtherTalk.
atprint: printing on weka1:LaserWriter@East_Ora_
EtherTalk.
[ 3 pages * 1 copy ] left in -
[dhcp-123-45:~/Desktop] chuck$
```

The *enscript* command is used to translate plain text into
PostScript so the file can be printed. The *atprint* command lets you stream any Unix output to an AppleTalk
printer. In this example, the commands are piped
together (using the standard Unix pipe, |), which for-
mats the file and sends it to the default AppleTalk
printer. Additional information about *enscript* and its
options can be found in its manpage (*man enscript*).

---

### TIP

There is another Unix facility, *lpd*, for printing from the
command line. However, configuring *lpd* is beyond the
scope of this book. For information on how to configure
*lpd* and use its associated commands (*lpr*, *lpq*, *lprm*), see
*Learning Unix for Mac OS X Panther* (O'Reilly).

---

## Maintenance and Troubleshooting

The following settings deal with maintenance and trouble-shooting issues:

*Force quit an application that's stuck?*

Option-⌘-Escape opens a window that shows all the running applications. Select the troublesome application and click the Force Quit button.

Option-click the application's icon in the Dock. A pop-up window will appear next to the icon with the Force Quit option; move the mouse over and release on that option.

Applications → Utilities → Process Viewer → select the process that's causing the problem → Processes → Quit Process.

*Restart my system when it's completely frozen?*

Hold down the Shift-Option-⌘ keys and press the Power-on button.

*Turn on crash reporting so I can see why an application crashed?*

Applications → Utilities → Console → Preferences → Crashes panel; select both options. Now, when an application crashes, the Console app will automatically launch and display the cause of the crash.

*Where are crash logs kept?*

If you've enabled crash logging, crash logs will be stored in the *~/Library/Logs* directory.

*Fix a disk that won't mount?*

Applications → Utilities → Disk Utility → select the disk that won't mount → First Aid.

*My system completely froze after launching an application. What can I do?*

Follow these steps:

1. Do a hard restart of your system: Control-⌘-Power-on (or Eject).

---

2. Log back into your system.

3. Launch the Terminal (*/Applications/Utilities*).

4. Enter the following command and hit Return:

   ```
   [MacPanther:~] chuck$ sudo shutdown now
   ```

   This forces an automatic shutdown of your system and takes you into single-user mode. Your screen will go black and you'll be faced with a text prompt.

5. At the prompt, enter the following command:

   ```
   sh-2.05a# fsck -y
   ```

   The *fsck* command performs a filesystem check and reports back its findings:

   ```
   bootstrap_look_up( ) failed (ip/send) invalid
   destination port
   bootstrap_look_up( ) failed (ip/send) invalid
   destination port
   bootstrap_look_up( ) failed (ip/send) invalid
   destination port
   ** /dev/rdisk0s2
   ** Root file system
   ** Checking HFS Plus volume.
   ** Checking Extents Overflow file.
   ** Checking Catalog file.
   ** Checking multi-linked files.
   ** Checking Catalog hierarchy.
   ** Checking volume bitmap.
   ** Checking volume information.
   ** The volume MacPanther appears to be OK.
   sh-2.05a#
   ```

6. If *fsck -y* reports that the disk has been modified, you will need to run the command again until the filesystem checks out to be OK.

7. If everything is fine, enter *reboot* at the command prompt and hit Return to reboot your system.

*Partition a new hard drive?*

   Applications → Utilities → Disk Utility → select the new drive → Partition.

*Erase a CD-RW disc or hard drive?*

Applications → Utilities → Disk Utility → select the CD or disk → Erase.

*Create a redundant array of independent disks (RAID) for my system?*

Applications → Utilities → Disk Utility → select the drives → RAID.

*Access command-line mode and bypass Aqua?*

There are three ways you can access the command-line interface:

- Hold down ⌘-S when starting up the system; this is known as single-user mode.

- At the login window, type >*console* as the username, don't enter a password, and click on the Login button. This is known as multiuser mode and is just like being in the Terminal, except that your entire screen is the Terminal.

- From the Terminal, type *sudo shutdown now* and hit Return; this also places you in single-user mode.

When you've finished diagnosing your system, type *reboot* and press Return to reboot your system into Aqua.

*Rebuild Classic's desktop?*

System Preferences → Classic → Advanced panel. There is no need to rebuild Mac OS X's desktop, so holding down Option-⌘ keys at startup is futile.

*All the icons on my system look funny. Is there an easy way to fix this problem?*

Even though Mac OS X is more reliable than earlier versions of the Mac OS, icons and such can still go haywire. The quick fix for this problem is to delete the three "LS" files (*LSApplications*, *LSClaimedTypes*, and *LSSchemes*) in ~/*Library/Preferences*.

*There is a question mark icon in the Dock. What is this?*

A question mark icon in the Dock or in one of the tool-bars means that the application, folder, or file that the original icon related to has been deleted from your system. Just drag the question mark icon away from the Dock or toolbar to make it disappear.

*I have a dual-processor G4 machine. Can I see how efficiently the processors are distributing the workload?*

Applications → Utilities → CPU Monitor. Each processor will have its own meter bar.

*View a log of software updates?*

System Preferences → Software Update → Show Log.

*How do I connect an external monitor or projector to my PowerBook without restarting?*

Select  → Sleep to put your laptop to sleep, plug in and turn on the display, and then hit the Escape key to wake your system and the display. You can then use the Display System Preference (System Preferences → Display) to turn display mirroring on or off as needed.

# Special Characters

Included with Mac OS X is the Keyboard Viewer application, which is a keyboard widget that allows you to see which character would be created by applying the Shift, Option, or Shift-Option keys to any key on the keyboard. To enable Keyboard Viewer, go to System Preferences → International → Input Menu and select the checkbox next to Keyboard Viewer. The Input menu will appear in the menu bar; to launch the Keyboard Viewer, simple select this item from the Input menu.

While this might seem useful, it can be a hassle to launch another app just to create one character and copy and paste it into another program. Fortunately, one of the most little-known/-used features of the Mac OS is its ability to give you the same functionality within any application—making Keyboard Viewer unnecessary if you know what you're doing. Table 23 lists these special characters. Keep in mind that this doesn't work for all font types, and some fonts—such as Symbol, Wingdings, and Zapf Dingbats—create an entirely different set of characters or symbols. For example, to create the symbol for the Command key (⌘), you would need to switch the font to Wingdings and type a lowercase z.

*Table 23. Special characters and their key mappings*

| Normal | Shift | Option | Shift-Option |
|--------|-------|--------|--------------|
| 1 | ! | ¡ | ⁄ |
| 2 | @ | ™ | € |
| 3 | # | £ | ‹ |
| 4 | $ | ¢ | › |
| 5 | % | ∞ | fi |
| 6 | ^ | § | fl |
| 7 | & | ¶ | ‡ |
| 8 | * | • | ° |
| 9 | ( | ª | • |
| 0 | ) | º | ‚ |
| ` | ~ | Grave (`)[a] | ‘ |
| - (hyphen) | _ (underscore) | – (en-dash) | — (em-dash) |
| = | + | ≠ | ± |
| [ | { | " | " |
| ] | } | ' | ' |
| \ | \| | « | » |
| ; | : | … | Ú |
| ' | " | æ | Æ |
| , | < | ≤ | ¯ |
| . | > | ≥ | ˘ |
| / | ? | ÷ | ¿ |

*Table 23. Special characters and their key mappings (continued)*

| Normal | Shift | Option | Shift-Option |
|--------|-------|--------|--------------|
| a | A | å | Å |
| b | B | ∫ | ı |
| c | C | ç | Ç |
| d | D | ∂ | Î |
| e | E | Acute (´)[a] | ´ |
| f | F | ƒ | Ï |
| g | G | © | ˝ |
| h | H | ˙ | Ó |
| i | I | Circumflex (ˆ)[a] | ˆ |
| j | J | Δ | Ô |
| k | K | ° |  |
| l | L | ¬ | Ò |
| m | M | µ | Â |
| n | N | Tilde (˜)[a] | ˜ |
| o | O | ø | Ø |
| p | P | π | ∏ |
| q | Q | œ | Œ |
| r | R | ® | ‰ |
| s | S | ß | Í |
| t | T | † | ˇ |
| u | U | Umlaut (¨)[a] | ¨ |
| v | V | √ | ◊ |
| w | W | Σ | ˝ |
| x | X | ≈ | ˛ |
| y | Y | ¥ | Á |
| z | Z | Ω | ˛ |

[a] To apply this accent, you must press another key after invoking the Option-*key* command. See Table 24.

One thing you might have noticed in Table 23 is that when the Option key is used with certain letters, it doesn't necessarily create a special character right away; you need to press another character key to apply the accent. Unlike the other Option-key commands, when used with the ` (backtick), E, I, N, and U characters, you can create accented characters as shown in Table 24.

Table 24. Option-key commands for creating accented characters

| Key | Option-` | Option-E | Option-I | Option-N | Option-U |
|---|---|---|---|---|---|
| a | à | á | â | ã | ä |
| Shift-A | À | Á | Â | Ã | Ä |
| e | è | é | ê | ˜e | ë |
| Shift-E | È | É | Ê | ˜E | Ë |
| i | ì | í | î | ˜i | ï |
| Shift-I | Ì | Í | Î | ˜I | Ï |
| o | ò | ó | ô | õ | ö |
| Shift-O | Ò | Ó | Ô | Õ | Ö |
| u | ù | ú | û | ˜u | ü |
| Shift-U | Ù | Ú | Û | ˜U | Ü |

For example, to create the acute-accented e's in the word *résumé*, you would type Option-E and then press the E key. If you want an uppercase acute-accented E (É), press Option-E and then Shift-E. Try this out with various characters in different fonts to see what sort of characters you can create.

# Index

We'd like to hear your suggestions for improving our indexes. Send email to *index@oreilly.com*.

---

---

---

# Related Titles Available from O'Reilly

## Macintosh

AppleScript:
The Definitive Guide

Appleworks 6:
The Missing Manual

The Best of the Joy of Tech

iMovie 3 and iDVD:
The Missing Manual

iPhoto2: The Missing Manual

iPod: The Missing Manual

Mac OS X Panther in a Nutshell

Mac OS X: The Missing Manual,
*Panther Edition*

Mac OS X Unwired

Macintosh Troubleshooting
Pocket Guide

Office X for the Macintosh:
The Missing Manual

Running Mac OS X Panther

Switching to the Mac

## Mac Developers

Building Cocoa Applications:
A Step-By-Step Guide

Cocoa in a Nutshell

Learning Carbon

Learning Cocoa with
Objective-C, *2nd Edition*

Learning Unix for
Mac OS X Panther

Mac OS X for Java Geeks

Mac OS X Hacks

Mac OS X Panther for
Unix Geeks

Objective-C Pocket Reference

Programming Quartz 2D

RealBasic: The Definitive
Guide, *2nd Edition*

# Keep in touch with O'Reilly

## 1. Download examples from our books

To find example files for a book, go to:
*www.oreilly.com/catalog*

select the book, and follow the "Examples" link.

## 2. Register your O'Reilly books

Register your book at *register.oreilly.com*

Why register your books? Once you've registered your O'Reilly books you can:

- Win O'Reilly books, T-shirts or discount coupons in our monthly drawing.
- Get special offers available only to registered O'Reilly customers.
- Get catalogs announcing new books (US and UK only).
- Get email notification of new editions of the O'Reilly books you own.

## 3. Join our email lists

Sign up to get topic-specific email announcements of new books and conferences, special offers, and O'Reilly Network technology newsletters at:
*elists.oreilly.com*

It's easy to customize your free elists subscription so you'll get exactly the O'Reilly news you want.

## 4. Get the latest news, tips, and tools
*www.oreilly.com*

- "Top 100 Sites on the Web"—PC Magazine
- CIO Magazine's Web Business 50 Awards

Our web site contains a library of comprehensive product information (including book excerpts and tables of contents), downloadable software, background articles, interviews with technology leaders, links to relevant sites, book cover art, and more.

## 5. Work for O'Reilly

Check out our web site for current employment opportunities:
*jobs.oreilly.com*

## 6. Contact us

O'Reilly & Associates, Inc.
1005 Gravenstein Hwy North
Sebastopol, CA 95472 USA

TEL: 707-827-7000 or 800-998-9938
(6am to 5pm PST)

FAX: 707-829-0104

**order@oreilly.com**
For answers to problems regarding your order or our products.
To place a book order online, visit:
*www.oreilly.com/order_new*

**catalog@oreilly.com**
To request a copy of our latest catalog.

**booktech@oreilly.com**
For book content technical questions or corrections.

**corporate@oreilly.com**
For educational, library, government, and corporate sales.

**proposals@oreilly.com**
To submit new book proposals to our editors and product managers.

**international@oreilly.com**
For information about our international distributors or translation queries. For a list of our distributors outside of North America check out:
*international.oreilly.com/distributors.html*

**adoption@oreilly.com**
For information about academic use of O'Reilly books, visit:
*academic.oreilly.com*

---

# O'REILLY®

Our books are available at most retail and online bookstores.
To order direct: 1-800-998-9938 • *order@oreilly.com* • *www.oreilly.com*
Online editions of most O'Reilly titles are available at *safari.oreilly.com*